"I have seen many people ~~~~~~~~~~~~~~
that would strongly benefit ~~~~~~~~~~~
idea how to conduct thems~~~~~~~~~~~~~~~~,
living arrangements, lines of credit, and their effect on other peoples'
lives. People that are transitioning from high school to the adult world
should read this during their student career."

                Sergeant Jason D. Paul – *United States Marine Corps*

"What I liked most was that each subject was long enough for the
details needed, but not too long to lose interest."

                Jennifer Paul – *actress, wife, mom and daughter*

"I definitely think you're doing a service for young adults with this!"

                Eve Gumpel – *owner Good Writing Matters*

Shifting to the Business of Life

"Failure to prepare, is preparing for failure."
John Wooden – *former head basketball coach, UCLA*

No part of this publication may be reproduced, stored in a retrieval system or transmitted in any form by any means: Electronic, mechanical, photocopying, recording or otherwise without prior written permission of the author, except for excerpts quoted from resources.

Copyright 2015
Janet M. Nast

JANET M. NAST

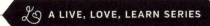
A LIVE, LOVE, LEARN SERIES

Shifting *to the* Business *of* Life

A Survival Guide for Young Adults

COVER DESIGN BY:
NICTE CREATIVE DESIGN, LLC.

Dedication

Alan, Jenn, Jason and Vic – All your questions made me do it.

Acknowledgments

A lot of very special people helped me get this book off the ground, starting–as always–with my kids, Jennifer and Alan. They are two amazing young adults who kept my being a single parent from being worse than it could have been. As a result, they (and their friends) are always coming to me with questions . . . which are now all answered in one place: This book.

And I couldn't do any writing without my husband Tom, who continues to love and support me by keeping the house and our world running while I type like a crazy lady every minute of every day. He is truly a gift from God for whom I am extremely grateful.

A big thank you goes to my friends Tim Prince and Galene Thayer along with my wonderful coworkers at the Ken Blanchard Companies, Terry Orletsky, Dana Kyle, Janey Feuer, Anila Verma, Sharon Hermann, and Steve Jack, who all took the time to review this material for content and accuracy and, in turn, prevented me from making some potentially embarrassing mistakes. I am so very grateful for their hard work.

I thank and appreciate Peter Gray for knocking around book titles with me and helping me to get my message across by using all the right words.

Thank you to my wonderful and talented copy editor, Eve Gumpel, for her expertise in grammar and punctuation, the time she took to look things up that didn't cross my mind, and her creative writing skills. When I couldn't come up with a good way to say something, she always could. And for that I am eternally grateful!

Dick Knuth has been instrumental in my getting this book published. I can't thank him enough for all his technical help, his kind and encourging words and, most importantly, his unlimited amount of patience with me.

Lastly, I'd like to thank all the friends I've been able to keep in touch with over the years via Facebook: Shirley Amos, Cheryl Owen, Ron Badour, Katie Carter, Jack Carter, Sandy Callis, Kellie Hurst Jones, Galene Thayer, Vicki Fair, Susan Kreiner, Ana Paul, Pam Rowe, Jennifer Paul, Sgt. Jason Paul, Mark Smitz, Dasia Gonzales, Jeff Horton, Ira Perot, Sabrina Reesor, Ann Ellsworth Parks, and Shelley Piroy. They were all kind enough to help me make decissions regarding the book cover and author pictures when I was just too close to the project be objective. I think they did good, and I hope you all agree!

Table of Contents

Legal Documents..17
    Social Security Number and Card............................19
    Identity Theft...21
    Driver's License...22
    Passport..24
Social Issues..25
    Registering to Vote...25
    Jury Duty..26
    Law Enforcement..28
        Officers of the Law..28
Sex..31
    Statutory Rape..31
    STDs..33
    Pregnancy...34
Cell Phones..35
    Contracts: Voice, Data, Text....................................36
Employment...37
    Minimum Wage..37
    Full-Time vs. Part-Time Jobs...................................37
    Hourly vs. Salary..38
    Overtime...39
    Gross Pay vs. Net Pay..39
    Applications..40
    Résumés..41
    Your Internet Presence...43
Job Interview...45
    Employer Homework..45
    What to Wear..46
    Tattoos and Piercings...47
    What to Bring With You..47
    What Not to Say...48
    Acceptable Answers/Interview Question..................48
Employer Benefits..49

Shifting to the Business of Life

- Health, Dental, Vision Care Insurance...50
- Co-Pays...51
- Flex Plan Accounts..52
- Retirement...55
  - Beneficiaries...55
  - Retirement Accounts...56
  - Social Security Accounts..56
  - Pensions..57
  - 401(k) vs. 401(k) Roth...58
- Income Taxes...63
  - W-2 Forms..64
  - Filing Income Tax Returns...64
  - Deductions/Write-Offs..65
  - Loopholes...66
- Bank Accounts..69
  - Beneficiaries...69
  - Checking Accounts...70
    - Overdraft...71
    - Stop Payments...72
    - Debit Cards..72
    - How to Write a Check..74
  - Savings Accounts..76
  - On-Line Banking...76
  - Balancing On-Line vs. Paper..77
- Budgeting...79
- Credit..83
  - Credit Scores...83
  - Why are Credit Scores Important?...86
  - How to Get Credit..86
  - Credit Cards: How Do You Get One?...88
  - How They Work..88
- Interest..91
  - Cost of the Loan...92
  - Fiscal Year vs. Calendar Year..93
  - APR...94

- No Interest for 24 Months...94
  - Balance Transfers...94
  - 24 Months Same as Cash...95
- Buying a Car/Vehicle...97
  - The Sticker Price...98
  - Used Cars...98
  - Car Insurance...99
    - Deductibles...101
  - Down Payments...102
  - Financing a Car Loan...102
    - Interest Rates on Car Loans...102
  - Purchase vs. Lease...104
  - Contracts/Purchase/Lease Agreements...105
  - Vehicle Warranties...106
  - Personal Vehicle Maintenance...108
  - Pink Slip...109
  - Registration at the DMV...110
- Selling a Car/Vehicle...111
  - Kelley Blue Book...111
  - Sell/Trade to Dealer...113
  - Sell It Yourself...114
    - Safety Issues...115
  - The Sale Process...116
  - Transferring Pink Slips...116
- Marriage...119
  - Prenuptial Agreement...120
  - Marriage License...121
  - The Wedding...121
  - Changing Names...122
    - Social Security Card...122
    - Driver's License...123
    - Income Tax Filing Options...123
- Housing...125
  - Costs...125
  - Rent/Mortgage...125

- Moving Expenses..126
- Ongoing Living Expenses..126
- Utilities...127
- Preparing to Move...128
  - 30 Days' Notice to Vacate..128
    - Exceptions: Military..129
    - Exceptions: Other...129
  - Collecting Boxes and Packing Materials.....................129
  - Packing Your Belongings...130
  - Getting Utilities Turned On/Off...................................132
  - Submitting Change of Address....................................133
  - Arrange to Transport Your Belongings.......................134
- Renting an Apartment..135
  - Renter's Insurance..135
  - Rental/Lease Agreements...136
  - Roommates...137
  - Month-to-Month vs. Lease...138
- Renting a House...139
  - Other Issues and Costs...140
- Purchasing a House..143
  - New vs. Used..143
  - New Houses/Condos...144
  - Home Loans..145
    - Fixed Rates vs. Variables...146
  - Property Taxes..148
    - Supplemental Property Taxes..................................148
    - Mello-Roos..149
  - Used Houses/Condos..149
  - Homeowner's Associations..150
  - Homeowner's Insurance...151
  - Impound Accounts..152
- Divorce...153
  - Filing Income Taxes After a Divorce..........................155
- Appendix A...157

Shifting to the Business of Life

Amortization Schedule 157
Appendix B 161
   Balancing a Checkbook 161
Appendix C 165
   Supplies for Your First Apartment 165
Appendix D 169
   Supplies for Your First House 169
Final Thoughts 171

Disclaimer

All the information contained on these pages came from my own life experiences and from my own brain. I do not profess to be a doctor, lawyer, tax accountant or bookkeeper.

However, I've been gainfully employed with various companies for over 40 years (starting out with a few minimum-wage jobs); bought and leased a variety of vehicles; rented, leased and bought a few condos and houses; been a landlord; raised two children as a single mom; been married four times and divorced three times. With all my life experience, you can bet the material about which I've written paints a pretty accurate picture of how things are done as of the date this book was published.

That said, use this book as a guide – and then do your own homework for any situation you might be facing. Look it up on the Internet, and talk to professional doctors, lawyers, tax accountants or bookkeepers for the exact answers. I don't know everything – and neither does anyone else!

Legal Documents

One of the first things to understand about turning 18 is that anything you sign from that day forward is a legal commitment that you will do whatever you agreed to in that document. Thus, it's a legal document. You will see soon enough how many pieces of paper people will put in front of you with a pen in hand saying, "Sign here." Don't take that lightly: Read these documents before you sign them. Folks have lost court battles over signed contracts where the signer didn't read the "fine print" and had no idea what he or she agreed to. Judges don't want to hear you say, "I didn't know."

And be careful: Something new that the cell phone companies seemed to have started is "verbal contracts," although I've dealt with insurance companies that do the same thing. This is where the sales rep and you have a discussion about what you want or don't want. Then, at the end

Shifting to the Business of Life

of that discussion, they summarize it for you, ask if you agree, and then have you sign on the dotted line.

When this process is done over the phone, at least they let you know that the call is being recorded. So if push comes to shove, you can ask for a copy of the recording. But, in some cases when it's done face to face, there is no recording. Scary, isn't it? I'm not wild about this but it appears to be the only way to get anything done with some companies.

While I've provided details throughout this handbook for specific types of legal documents you will come across in various situations such as buying a car or leasing an apartment, you can check out this short list just to wrap your mind around the many types of documents that can be legally enforced in a court of law when you add your signature.

- Cell phone contracts
- Car purchase or lease agreements
- Any form where you specify a "beneficiary" (the person who gets/inherits all your money and/or belongings when you die) such as a retirement account or life insurance
- Credit card applications
- Employee work contracts
- Bank account forms/signature cards
- Apartment rental or lease agreements
- Home purchase agreements
- Passports
- Medical forms

Social Security Number and Card

It is a law that all citizens of the United States have a unique nine-digit Social Security number. This number connects every legal transaction and legal process in which you get involved throughout your entire life.

Your parents were required to get a Social Security number (and card) for you the minute you were born. They need it to get medical insurance for you and to claim you on their income taxes (as a dependent) until you are 18 years old.

No, you do not need it to get a driver's license. If someone asks for it at the Department of Motor Vehicles, go to another window or ask for a supervisor and report that.

After you turn 18 ask your parents for your card (and guard it with your life) because you will need it for every legal document you ever fill out and sign for the rest of your life. (Many are explained throughout this handbook.)

This number allows all insurance companies, banks (and other financial institutions such as loan companies), government agencies (city, state and federal) and employers to keep track of what (if any) services you are using, how much money you are putting into your Social Security retirement account (see Page 56 for more information about Social Security accounts), how much money you make and how much you owe and pay in taxes.

When you apply for a job, a loan, an apartment, or a credit card you will be required to provide this number. Make sure the company to

Shifting to the Business of Life

which you are applying for any of these items is a legitimate company. If you are not sure, go to an older friend whom you trust or seek your parent's advise. You should also research it on the Internet. If you're still in doubt, walk away from this transaction.

Read more information regarding how your Social Security number defines who you are in the section titled "Credit Scores" on Page 83.

Identity Theft

Never give out your Social Security number to anyone on the Internet, via email, or over the phone unless you initiated the call or transaction. If it seems a fishy situation, go with your gut feeling; if anything, err on the side of caution.

Never allow anyone else use of your Social Security number for anything: Not your parents (unless you are in college and they are still covering you for insurance and taxes), friends, or any other person.

If someone else gets your number they can "become you" on paper. This is called "identity theft." That means they can now open credit cards in your name, run up the balance and then not pay. They can take advantage of your health insurance and get into your checking account, apply for a job, or even buy a car in your name.

Driver's License

While this might seem to be a no-brainer, I've run into quite a few kids who don't have a driver's license and don't seem to want one. At 16, my son didn't feel the need to have one because he didn't want to drive. He thought I could just keep driving him everywhere. Really?

However, a driver's license is your second – and therefore, most important – form of legal identification right after your birth certificate. It has a picture of you, your current address, height, weight, hair and eye color, and your signature. The same cannot be said about your birth certificate, your student ID or your library card.

You will need a driver's license to do most or all of the following:

- Get a job
- Get a credit card
- Use a credit card
- Apply for any loan
- Rent an apartment or house
- Rent a stroller in the mall
- Rent a horse
- Drive a car
- Board an airplane

The earliest age at which you can get one in most states is 16. Check with your DMV to find out your state's laws. You will need to bring your birth certificate (or passport if you have one – see Page 24) with you in order to get it.

You must have your license with you when driving but it's best to have it with you at all times since it will be your main form of identification. So keep it in your wallet.

Driver's licenses are renewed every three to five years. Again, check with your local DMV for specific laws and guidelines in your state.

> *<u>Note:</u> The DMV also issues identification cards that look similar to a driver's license, but are for identification purposes only.*

Passport

A passport is required anytime you travel outside the country. Rather than a document, a passport is a little book, approximately 3.5 by 5 inches, usually navy blue in color, containing a picture of you, your current address and multiple pages where each customs officer will place a stamp as you "go through customs" upon entering a new country.

You can apply for a passport at most US Post Offices. Anyone can get one at any age. In order to get one you must have your birth certificate, approximately $120, and a nice smile because you must have your picture taken. You don't need a driver's license although the postal representative will take a look at it as a second form of identification. A driver's license isn't required because everyone who wants to travel to another country, including babies and children, must have a passport and children don't have drivers' licenses.

Be sure to allow up to six months for your request to be processed. If all is well in the world, you could receive a new passport (in the mail) in as little as four weeks. On the other hand, if your destination is undergoing political unrest or is perceived as a threat to the United States, it could take up to six months: So plan ahead.

Social Issues

Registering to Vote

Voting for the President of the United States is one of the greatest privileges of being a citizen of the United States. Even better, you can stay informed about political issues in your city, state, or the nation, and express your opinion about those issues to the politicians who represent you. In many cases, you'll also have the opportunity to vote on issues that affect you.

In order to vote you must be a legal citizen of the USA and you need to register to vote. You can register at any US Post Office, at some libraries and, any time a big election is coming up, you will find people in the mall or grocery stores who will register you.

Jury Duty

Another great privilege we have as citizens is having the right to convict, or not convict, anyone who is accused of being a criminal. That is called being on a "jury of one's peers."

In order to get selected for jury duty, many states require you to have a valid driver's license. But in some states the courts might select potential jury members from among those who have paid taxes, purchased a home or registered to vote. It varies from state to state.

When you receive a "summons to appear," you may or may not be selected to serve on a jury. (You can also request a postponement if you cannot fulfill your commitment on the date your summons specifies.) Generally speaking, the selection is done through a process of elimination that looks something like this:

First, you will report in to the court on the date specified [on your summons] along with 200 + other people. (In some states, your summons will direct you to call in to "report" rather than physically show up – so read your summons for your specific instructions.)

When you check in you will be asked about any hardships this might cause you or your family, or if there is any other reason you cannot serve at this time.

- If serving on a jury at this time will cause some sort of hardship, you will be released from service and sent home. At that point, your "duty" is done for that year.

Shifting to the Business of Life

- If you have no [valid] reason to not serve, then you wait until the judge calls you for the next steps. You are now in what is called the "jury pool."

Next, there is a 50/50 chance of being called into a courtroom by a judge.

- If you are not called in, usually by noon, then you will be sent home and, again, your "duty" is done for that year.

When you are called in to the courtrom, the judge and the lawyers will then randomly select twelve potential jury members to take a seat in the jury box. They will ask each person a series of questions to determine if he or she is a good fit for the case being tried.

- If you are not selected (they won't tell you why not) you will be sent home right way. Your "duty" is done for that year.
- If you are selected, they will tell you how long the trial is expected to last and then ask again if this will cause a hardship: If not, you are there for the duration; if yes, you will be sent home right way. Your "duty" is done for that year.

Law Enforcement

Now that you are legally considered an "adult," it's in your best interest to follow some guidelines whenever you find yourself face-to-face with any law enforcement officer. Before getting into the details, I'll begin by saying there are two basic rules:

1. Always follow orders
2. Always be respectful by addressing any officer of the law with "Yes Sir; No Sir" or "Yes Ma'am; No Ma'am."

Just so you're clear on what "Officer of the Law" means, I've included a list of possible titles along with some behavior guidelines (on the next page) that include common orders an officer might give.

Officers of the Law

Here are some titles I've come across over the years. This list is not all-inclusive but should give you a good idea.

- Police Officer
- Sheriff
- Highway Patrol Officer
- Probation Officer
- Corrections Officer
- Security Guard
- FBI, CIA agents
- Detective
- Undercover Agent
- Officers of the Court, aka, Probation Officer, Bailiff

Some slang terms might include:

- Cop
- Rent-A-Cop
- Po Po
- Fuzz
- Pig

Shifting to the Business of Life

When Confronted by an Officer of the Law

Regardless of how you refer to officers of the law, always remember that they have the power and the law on their side, and in many cases, they have a gun. With that in mind, when they give you an order to do something you should always do as they say, do it with a smile, and say "Yes Sir; No Sir" or "Yes Ma'am; No Ma'am."

Here are some examples of the orders an officer might give you:

- "Stop, this is the police!" (You could be walking, running, driving or riding a bike.)
- "Don't move!" (While you might be walking, running, driving or riding a bike, you could also be sitting in your car during a traffic stop.)
- "Pull over." (Indicated by the red lights flashing in your review mirror when you are driving.)
- "License and registration." (This is common if you are stopped while driving.)
- "Put your hands on the wheel." (This is also common if you are stopped while driving.)
- "Get out of the car."
- "Show me your hands." (Always keep your hands in view unless told otherwise.)
- "Put your hands on your head."
- "Lie down on the ground."
- "Drop your weapon." (This is the most dangerous of situations. Even if you are only holding a toy gun such as a BB gun, do as you are told immediately! The officer cannot always tell a real weapon from a toy weapon at first glance, so if the officer feels in

---

Shifting to the Business of Life

that one split second that his life is in danger, he might shoot first and ask questions later.)
- "Get up against the car."

As you can see in most of these situations, you run the risk of getting hurt if you don't do as you are told immediately. You never know if this officer is looking for someone else and you are just in the wrong place at the wrong time, or if she's just been in a bad situation with someone else before you crossed her path.

Besides running the risk of getting hurt, there is also that formal charge referred to as, "failing to comply" or "resisting arrest." If this occurs, you can be arrested, thrown in the back of a police car and taken to jail while they work out the "details" later. This type of charge may or may not stick depending upon the situation, but if it does here are some possible long-term results:

- Jail time
- A court hearing in front of a judge
- A monetary fine (And if you don't pay, your wages could be garnished by the state.)
- A permanent arrest record which can follow you around for the rest of your life. (Yes, in some cases this record can be "expunged," aka, erased. Talk with a lawyer to find out for sure.)
- Probation (The release of an offender from detention, subject to a period of good behavior while under supervision by an officer of the court, aka, probation officer.)
- And the worst thing of all, you could lose your job if your employer gets wind of this situation.

Enough said!

Sex

While this is not a book about sex, as an adult you should be aware of all the long-term medical issues as well as legal issues that can rear their ugly head with regards to sex. So I'll briefly define a few things here and then strongly suggest you either ask a doctor or lawyer for more facts.

Statutory Rape

Depending upon the state in which you live, when you turn 18 you are legally considered an "adult" in the eyes of the law. Do not have sex with anyone under the age of 18 (aka a "minor"). Doing so is called "Statutory Rape" and it is illegal. If said minor's parents want to, they can have you arrested and thrown in jail. When that happens your name will be added to the list of "Registered Sex Offenders" (aka, child molesters) in your state, forever!

Shifting to the Business of Life

Yes, I understand you were 18 and your girlfriend or boyfriend was 16, and you were both "there" because you wanted to be, and at 16 he/she was pretty mature. But, the law doesn't care!

"Forever" means just what it says: There is no way on earth (that I know of) this can be removed from your permanent criminal record.

What this also means (forever) is that any potential employer will find this very public record about you simply by doing a quick search for "Megan's Law" on the Internet. (That's the law that makes child molesters' records public.)

Bottom line: Always remember that in most states, having sex with anyone under (legal) age is illegal and there is no getting around it!

> *Tip:* *I'm not familiar with the age restriction laws in all states or countries, so look it up before you do something stupid.*

STDs

"STD" means a Sexually Transmitted Disease. These include (but are not limited to) AIDS, HIV, herpes, Chlamydia, syphilis and gonorrhea. Yes, you can catch any or all of these regardless if you are straight or gay, and yes, you can catch any or all of them the first time you have sex.

Some of these, such as AIDS and HIV can kill you. Some, such as herpes, won't kill you, but it will make you miserable for the rest of your life because there is no cure. (What's more, I don't think anyone will spend any time looking for a cure because herpes is just a nasty little inconvenience from which no one has died.)

So yes, you should use a condom every time you have sex (aka, protected sex). And, ladies, taking birth control pills is not "protected sex." Those protect you from unwanted pregnancy, not diseases. There are no exceptions no matter what your friends or older relatives tell you.

Something to consider when you begin a new relationship is for both of you to get screened, or tested, for STDs right away. Some STDs don't present symptoms right away so the only way you can really know for sure is to get tested.

Pregnancy

Yes, you can get pregnant the first time you have sex if you do it without some sort of birth control. If you are on birth control pills, no, you cannot miss one pill and still be safe.

I wouldn't count on any of the popular "tricks" either such as "pulling out" or thinking that certain days of the month before or after your period, are "safe." ***Again, there are no exceptions no matter what your friends or older relatives tell you.***

So before you jump into the sack with that special someone with whom you have such "amazing chemistry," do some research and make sure you are prepared for all of the physical consequences.

Cell Phones

While you can probably purchase a cell phone for under $100, personal cell phone service accounts are not cheap. (A cell phone does not work without the cell service.) They can run from $50 to $100 a month for a single phone number. It all depends on the minutes and data you think you'll use every month.

Yes, you can get a cell phone account in your own name without having established any credit, but it will require a hefty security deposit. (Refer to Page 83 to learn about credit.) And the cell phone company will hold onto your deposit for a year, minimum. After all, it's allowing you to use its cell service month-to-month, before you pay for it. So it's like paying for six months to a year up front. At the end of that year though, you'll receive a refund check for your full deposit amount.

Contracts: Voice, Data, Text

I've only had experience with my own cell company so I cannot speak for all of them. Do some research before you decide to get a cell phone.

Some companies offer no contract, one-year contracts, and two-year contracts. But what's funny about these "contracts" is that I've never seen one in writing that includes all the details as to how many minutes or text messages you're allowed or how much data you can use each month. Most of this "agreement" is verbal (whether I'm in the store or on the phone with a salesperson). But if I'm in the store and the salesperson prints out a long-ass receipt, it does say that if I try to cancel the contract, I will be charged up to $500 for that offense. ***So watch out: Read all your receipts!***

That said, I've noticed that my provider now puts a lot of this information in my "online" account. Which means I had to create an online account to see it. There's even a little phone app that I can conveniently put on my cell phone that gives me access to all my account information at the tap of a finger. Ask your provider if they have a such an app.

Employment

Yep, if you want to live on your own one day, you really do need to get a job. The next few sections describe a few things you should know about the process.

Full-Time vs. Part-Time Jobs

When you work 40 hours a week you are working "full-time." In general, anything less than 40 hours in a single week is considered a "part-time" job.

Minimum Wage

The "minimum wage" is the lowest amount of money (hourly wage) an employer can legally pay an employee. This amount varies from state to state and in some cases, from city to city.

Expect your first few jobs to pay minimum wage. To find out what that is, search for "minimum wage" for your state on the Internet.

As you move from one job to another and gain experience, your pay should go up.

> *Tip: No one "owes" you a living or anything else, nor do employers think you "deserve" anything more than what they are offering. You are only "special" to your parents.*

If you get a college education, you might get lucky and someone will hire you (on your first job) for a little more than minimum wage, but don't expect it just because you put all that time and money into a higher education. That is your issue, not your employer's.

> *Tip: Experience trumps education every time. Having both will help you to get ahead: So suck it up and take the low paying jobs at the start of your career.*

Hourly vs. Salary

Hourly workers are paid by the hour. For example, if you work 36 hours in one week, then you will get paid for 36 hours. Hourly workers are usually eligible to be paid overtime based upon the OT description on the next page.

Salaried workers get paid a set dollar amount per year, which is then divided by the number of pay periods in that year. For example, if your salary is $50,000 per year, and you get paid twice a month, (26 pay periods) then your net pay would be $1923.08 for each pay period. However, salaried workers do not get paid OT, no matter how many hours worked in a day or week.

Gross Pay vs. Net Pay

Gross pay is what you start out with before deductions.
Net pay is the amount of money that remains after income taxes (Page 63), Social Security (Page 56), and other deductions (see Employer Benefits on Page 49) are subtracted from your paycheck.

Overtime (OT)

Any amount of time you work over eight hours a day, or 40 hours in one week is considered overtime, also known as "OT."

Some companies will pay you time and a half for OT, and some will pay you double time. Time and a half looks like this: If you earn an hourly wage of $10 an hour, your overtime pay is $15 an hour for overtime. Double time would be $20 an hour.

Shifting to the Business of Life

Applications

This is the form you have to fill out to apply for a job. Every employer will ask you to do this. It will require that you provide the following information:

Name, Address, Phone Number
Email Address

Previous work experience: If you have none, leave this blank. Don't worry; zero employment history is not uncommon for folks under the age of 22 or 23. Most employers know that many people do not hold paying jobs, or jobs relating to their field of study, while in college.

Education: If you have not yet completed your education, be it high school or college, just enter the start date and leave the finish date blank or write in the words "in progress."

Don't lie on a job application. You can get fired when it's discovered. And yes, it will be discovered.

Résumés

A résumé is a document you create that contains essentially the same information as a job application. The difference is that you can add more information about your experience under each former employer. This is the place where you can really talk yourself up. Shown here is a sample résumé.

WORK EXPERIENCE

Janet M. Nast
42106 Chestnut Drive
Temecula, CA 92591
cell: (909)501-1333

Client Coordinator/Client Partnering Coordinator
The Ken Blanchard Companies
- Coordinate all activities for setting up client seminars from initial contracts to ordering "off the shelf materials" as well as custom materials
- Enter all client and sales reps promo orders in Navision: includes product orders as well as registrations for seminars, workshops and special events
- Answer all client inquiries from tracking shipments to invoicing issues
- Assist in drafting client contracts by working closely with the Office of Intellectual Property
- Format contracts, proposals, PowerPoint presentations and client lists in Excel
- Assemble and mail out marketing materials based upon client needs and marketing events
- Perform client research using online search engines such as Hoovers and Zap.com
- Update and maintain client information in our Siebel database
- Maintain an up-to-date familiarity with the extensive Ken Blanchard Product Line
- Contribute to the documentation and consistency of processes for Client Coordinators
- Create outlines for Siebel and Navision training
- Provide Siebel training & voice mail training for new hires within the department
- Provide assistance as needed in Microsoft products such as Outlook, Excel, Word and PowerPoint within the department
- Provide general PC troubleshooting within the department

Help Desk Technician/Instructor
The Ken Blanchard Companies
- Troubleshoot all software/hardware calls
- Contribute to the New Employee Orientation Program
- Provide 1-on-1 instruction for the MS Office products
- Develop software training programs & supporting documentation

Senior Software Instructor
SHARPER EXECUTIVE
EXECUTRAIN OF SAN DIEGO
LEARNSOFT INC.
- Conducted 1-2 day classes for a variety of end user applications
- Conducted private consultations with clients regarding their use of end user applications
- Designed, developed, published and implemented custom courseware
- Responsible for hardware and software classroom setup
- Responsible for trouble-shooting hardware and software issues as they presented themselves

Technical Documentation Specialist
MITCHELLMATIX, a division of Mitchell International
This position/dept. was created based upon my recommendation of the cost savings to the company:

You can also add any "special skills or talents" you may have. Only list things that would have something to do with the job for which you are applying.

For instance, if you know how to use MS Excel and you're applying for an admin assistant or data entry role, then add it. I don't know that I would bother to add that I know how to play five-card draw for either of those jobs. But if you're in Vegas, go for it.

Many websites offer guidance on how to type up a good résumé. Do some homework on this topic and learn well. (You can also hire someone to write your résumé.) When you think you have a good first draft, have a few professional people (not your parents or friends – they all think you are wonderful and may not be brutally honest with you) review it for you before you send it to potential employers. Your résumé can make the difference as to whether or not you get the job.

Your Internet Presence

Most employers will do some sort of "background" check on you and most of it can and will be done on the Internet. Your "Internet presence" refers to your Facebook, LinkedIn, Pinterest, Instagram, Twitter and every other online account you might have.

Potential employers will find your credit score (which reveals your financial history), all your education, and previous work experience. They will also find out about any illegal or criminal activity in which you might have engaged in your reckless youth.

> *Tip:* *Everything about anyone can be found on the Internet whether you like it or not. So you, or your parents, should be thinking of this the moment you first touch a computer.*

Job Interview

This is when your potential employer contacts you to arrange a meeting, or a phone interview, to get to know you. They liked what they saw on your job application or your résumé and want to know more: Do you look professional, can you carry on an intelligent conversation, and will you get along with other employees? The next few sections describe a few things to keep in mind when preparing for an interview.

Employer Homework

Get on the Internet and look up the company for which you want to work. Find out things like what the business does to make money, how big the company is (how many employees, how much money it makes in a year, in how many states or countries it has offices) and any other interesting tidbits of information such as the company culture and any "buzz words" they might use. Pictures can help give you an idea of how employees dress; perhaps you can also see examples of how they interact with each other or clients.

This type of information might just come up in the interview and you don't want to look like an idiot.

What to Wear

Rule No. 1: "It's better to be overdressed than underdressed."

Again, do some homework: You might be able to get an idea by looking up the company on the Internet. Ideally, you will find pictures of employees. The other option is to drive by the company and look at employees in the parking lot. *If neither option works, then go with Rule No. 1 above.* If you really aren't sure, it's always best to err on the more conservative side. Here are a few general guidelines:

- Women, stick with conservative necklines, skirt and dress hemlines to the knees and nothing sleeveless unless covered by a jacket. Solid colors are the most business-like. Also, keep your accessories simple.
- Men, go with slacks, shirt and a tie. No wild prints or words written on the tie. Add a jacket that can be removed if you find that your (male) interviewer is not wearing one.

There are many Internet sites that offer tips on how to put forth a more professional image: Take the time to look at a few.

Tattoos and Piercings

Yeah, they seem pretty cool to you and your friends. But unless you plan on working for your friends or relatives, or having minimum-wage jobs for the rest of your life, I strongly suggest you have these things done on a body part that is easily covered.

Take a minute to think about who runs and works for the companies for which you want to work; they are usually people in their 30s and up. The paying customers of those companies are around that age too, if not older. If it's a very successful business then management probably wants all of its employees to look professional. That is to say, to look like the majority of the paying customers it serves. And guess what? The majority of paying customers don't have nose rings, eyebrow piercings or extreme tattoos.

Argue all you want, but this is the way it is in the business world. So, downplay the unusual piercings and cover the tattoos.

What to Bring With You

- A pen
- A notepad
- A turned off cell phone
- Your driver's license and your Social Security card – Used for identification and payroll taxes only after you have been offered a job.

Shifting to the Business of Life

What Not to Say

- Don't ask to "borrow a pen" to fill out an application or take notes. (Refer to previous section, "What to Bring with You.")
- Don't bad-mouth your previous employer, boss or coworkers.
- Don't say those people weren't ready for your amazing ideas (too arrogant).
- Don't talk about how you couldn't get along with someone, regardless of the reason.

Acceptable Answers to the Most-Asked Interview Question

"Why did you, or are you, leaving your current employer?"

- I've heard a lot of great things about this company and I'm excited for (looking forward to) the opportunity to be a part of it.
- I'm relocating (moving to another city or state).
- I've gone as far as I believe I can go at (current company name) so I'm looking for more opportunities for growth in a company such as this. I've read, "this that and the other thing (fill in the blanks)," and I believe I can add to "blah blah blah (fill in the blanks)" part of the business and, at the same time, expand my skill set.

Employer Benefits

"Benefits" are services that some companies offer to their full-time (40 hours per week) employees. Most companies will not offer these services to part-time (fewer than 40 hours per week) employees.

Many of these services are included as part of an employee's salary. However some have small charges deducted from your paycheck such as health insurance. Here is a short list of some possible benefits an employer might offer:

- Health Insurance
- Dental Insurance
- Vision Care Insurance
- Retirement Accounts
- Flex Plans
- Sick Leave
- Paid Time Off (for vacations)

The only way to know for sure what kind of benefits your new employer offers is to ask your employer *after you have received a job offer.*

Health, Dental, Vision Care Insurance

Many companies will offer one or all three of these types of insurance. While health insurance coverage is pretty much mandatory since the Affordable Care Act was put into place, dental and vision insurance coverage are not. Also, employers are not required to pay the cost of any of these insurances. That said, many large companies will pay all or most of it. In the case where they don't pay for all of it, they will pass on a portion of the cost to you by taking regular deductions out of your paycheck.

Health insurance generally covers any doctors' visits you might make (due to injury or illness), the ongoing treatment of any illnesses you might have, the cost of yearly physical exams, as well as any surgeries you might need. Many will also now cover the cost of preventative care such as mammograms, blood tests, and "well woman" checkups. Check with the insurance carrier for details on exactly what your plan covers – it varies from one company to the next.

Dental insurance will usually cover part of the cost of a yearly checkup as well as minor repairs such as fillings for cavities and root canals, and major repairs such as crowns. Check with the insurance carrier for details on exactly what your plan covers – it varies from one company to the next.

Vision care will cover most of the cost of yearly eye exams, and a percentage of new lenses and frames. Some cover the cost of contact lenses. Check with the insurance carrier for details on exactly what your plan covers – it varies from one company to the next.

Co-pays

This is the dollar amount you will pay (in cash or credit) to a doctor's office at the time service is provided. For instance, there might be a $10 co-pay for a doctor's visit. Or a $250 co-pay for a surgery. When you sign up for insurance, be sure to read the section that outlines what the co-pays are for each service. If you have set up a flex plan account (see next section) with your company, you can use those dollars for co-pays.

Flex Plan Accounts

This is a "medical" savings account you can set up with your employer only. Not all employers offer it, and if yours does, you might or might not want to use it.

Each year during your "open enrollment" for employer sponsored health insurance you have the choice. At this time you can tell your employer to deduct any amount you want from your paycheck and put it into this "flex plan" account. I've put aside as little as $10 a paycheck and as much as $50 a paycheck.

Here are some general guidelines on how flex plans work:

The amount is deducted before income taxes are calculated. So your taxable income at the end of the year will be lower. This is a huge benefit that I take advantage of every year. Take a look at the following table to see what this could look like in regards to your take-home pay and your taxable income.

	With Flex Plan	No Flex plan
Annual Salary	$30,000	$30,000
$100 per mo. to Flex Plan	$1,200	$0
Taxable income amount	$28,800	$30,000
10% to taxes	$2,880	$3,000
Take home pay	$25,920	$27,000
Spendable income	$27,120	$27,000

Shifting to the Business of Life

When you add the flex plan dollars ($1,200) to your taxable income ($25,920) you find that you have $27,120 spendable income for the year, vs. $27,000. And you owe less in income taxes.

- Most plans require that the money be spent before the end of the calendar year in which it has been deducted, or you will lose it.
- The money can only be spent on government-approved medical expenses such as medical office co-pays, prescription medications, or medical deductibles. (Your employer must provide you with a list of approved expenses.)
- There is also a flex plan option that can be used for child day-care expenses.

Before you sign up for a flex plan account, think about it and do some math. For example, do you take any medications on a regular basis that cost you $10-$40 per month? Or do you see a chiropractor at the cost of $50 per visit that your insurance doesn't cover? Do you wear glasses and have limited or no insurance to pay for new ones the next year? Are you planning on any surgery or dental work in the next year that might have high deductibles? Do you pay for day-care for your kids?

If you answer "yes" to any of these questions, then see if your employer has a flex plan account and learn all you can about it.

Retirement

The younger you are when you begin to think about your retirement, the better off you will be when you get to that time of your life. I've heard it said that if you begin saving 10 percent of your income when you start working at age 21, you can have a $1,000,000 (yes, one million dollars!) saved by the time you retire at the age of 62. I'm no investment expert, but I'd say that that's worth looking into! So talk with your employer about their retirement options, or a financial planner (perhaps at your bank) and learn as much as you can about how to get the most out of retirement savings.

Beneficiaries

One thing to keep in mind as you consider setting up retirement accounts, is who you want your money to go to if you don't live long enough to collect it yourself. The person, or persons you specify are referred to as your "beneficiaries." If you are married with kids, you might select your wife or kids, or both. If you are single though, you might consider a close family member such as a sister or brother, or even a parent. Give this some thought as you are filling out the forms for these accounts.

Also keep in mind as your life's circumstances and status change, such as marriage or divorce, you should update your beneficiaries.

Retirement Accounts

Many employers offer the option of setting up and managing retirement accounts for you. There are many kinds of retirement accounts, but I'm only going to describe the four most common: Social Security, pension, 401(k), and 40K(k) Roth (aka Roth IRA).

When applying for a job, this is not something you would talk about in a first interview. You would ask about retirement accounts after a company has made you a job offer. It's something to seriously consider when deciding to accept said offer.

Social Security Accounts

This is the one your employer is required to set up by the federal government. Your Social Security account number is your Social Security number, which is why you need to give it to your employer. The payroll department will automatically deduct a certain amount (outlined in a chart by the government) from each paycheck you get and it will be deposited into your (government) Social Security account.

You cannot access this money until you turn 62, minimum. At age 62 you can apply (to the Social Security Administration) for it but you will only get a percentage of it. In other words, at 62 you might get 60 percent of what you're entitled to, at 65 you might collect 75 percent and at 68 you might collect 100 percent. I say "might," because I really don't know the exact age and percentage brackets. A tax accountant or financial planner can provide the exact numbers.

Pensions

This type of retirement account is set up and run by the company for which you work. Not many companies have pensions anymore. Pensions cost employers a lot of money, which is why so many no longer offer them. (Most offer 401(k) accounts, which are explained next.)

Here is basically how pensions work:

The employer deposits a certain amount of money into each employee's account each month for as long as the employee works for that company.

The employee can collect payments from his or her pension account after he or she has worked for the company a certain number of years and has reached retirement age. The company determines what the number of years is and what that age is.

If the company did a good job of guessing how long you will live after you retire, and what it will cost you to live and maintain your current lifestyle, you should be getting pension payments close to what your salary was, for the rest of your life. So you can see why a pension would cost an employer a lot of money. That's why many companies no longer do this.

401(k) vs. 401(k) Roth

What's really sad here is that I just recently learned the difference between the two of these and I'm 56 years old! You should know this sooner in life so that you make the best choice earlier in life when it really can make a difference. Both of these accounts can be set up and managed by your employer.

Here are some facts and differences between the two:

The 401(k) is money deducted from your paycheck before any federal and state income taxes, and Social Security are calculated and deducted. In the long run, that means that when you pull money out of your 401(k) account you have to pay taxes on it. This is referred to as "deferred" taxes. Surprisingly enough, this is not always a bad thing because when you retire, you no longer have that full-time, steady paycheck coming in, so your income is probably going to be a lot lower. Thus, you will pay lower income taxes.

As far as I know, only an employer can set this up because only your employer can get a hold of your paycheck before taxes. But ask someone in your Human Resources (HR) department, a tax accountant or a financial planner to be sure.

Money for a 401(k) Roth account is deducted from your paycheck after all federal and state deductions are taken out of your paycheck. That means that when you retire and start taking money out of this account, you do not have to pay taxes on it. Most employers and most banks can set this up for you since you cash your check and make deposits after taxes.

While a 401(k) Roth account might sound like a regular savings account, it's not. But it is similar to a 401(k) in these ways:

- You should not take money out of either a 401(k) or 401(k) Roth account until you reach retirement age (59.5 as of this writing.) If you make a withdrawal and do not pay it back (vs. a loan against it that must be paid back with after-tax money plus interest), you will have to pay a 10 percent penalty on that money. And, in the case of the 401(k), you would also have to pay the deferred income taxes.
- You can also decide where you want the money in these accounts to be invested over the years. That can be good because you have the potential of earning a lot more interest than just the 1 percent to 2 percent that savings accounts are currently paying.

The table (shown on the next page) is an example of three scenarios using nice, rounded numbers. It uses $50,000 per year as a salary, ten percent being deducted in taxes every year, and what your take-home pay could look like each year depending upon how you choose to save for retirement.

You can see in the first column, if you put 5 percent into a 401(k), that would be 5 percent of your $50,000 base salary, or $2,500, going into that account. Now you still have to pay 10 percent in income taxes, but it's 10 percent of $47,500, which is only $4,750 instead of $5000.

The example in the next column shows what it looks like if you choose not to save anything for retirement.

The third column shows what your income and then retirement account looks like if you choose to put that 5 percent into a 401(k) Roth account.

	401(k) Before taxes	No savings	401(k) Roth After taxes	
Annual Salary	$50,000	$50,000	$50,000	
5% Savings	$2,500	$0	$2,250	This 5% is calculated *after* the $5,000 is taken out in taxes.
Taxable income amount	$47,500	$50,000	50,000	
10 percent tax deduction	$4,750	$5,000	$5,000	
Take-home pay	$42,750	$45,000	$42,750	

On one hand, even though you'll have the same take home pay with a Roth 401(k), you aren't saving as much money. On the other hand, you are paying all your income taxes up front with the Roth 401(k) and you won't be taxed again later, like a regular 401(k).

While this is a simplified explanation of how these two accounts work, it gives you enough information to at least think about it and get started saving.

If you have questions about this and can't decide what you want to do, talk to your parents and see what they've done for their retirement. If they've done nothing then talk with an accountant or a financial planner. H & R Block might answer some basic questions for you for free. You can also look up terms such as "401(k)" and "401(k) Roth" on the Internet.

Whatever you decide, it's a smart idea to do something, and to begin as young as you can – even if it's only 1 percent of each paycheck. Who knows what kind of money you will have coming in when you're 65 or older? But with one of these options, you will at least have something.

Income Taxes

When you start getting a regular paycheck, money is deducted from each one by the payroll department where you work. One of those deductions is called "income taxes." State and federal governments use your taxes to maintain public infrastructure such as roads, jails, public buildings (libraries, government offices) and schools, as well as to pay the salaries of the people who do the work in those places. Taxes also pay the salaries of the politicians, aka, the people you elect to run the city and other government "businesses."

Yes, it's quite a shock the first time you get a paycheck and it's not what you calculated it would be based on the promised hourly wage multiplied by the number of hours you worked! But that's the way it is.

> ***Tip:*** *Refer to the section titled, "Filing Income Tax Returns" on the next page, for more information.*

W2 Forms

When you get your first job your employer will require you to fill out a "W-2" form. This is a form that tells the employer how much to deduct from your paycheck for income taxes.

The form will ask for your name and address, name of the employer and the number of "dependents" (children) you want to "claim." The number of dependents will help the government and your employer figure out how much you will owe in taxes at the end of the year.

Everyone is required to fill out a W-2 for federal income taxes. Depending upon where you live, you might also have to fill one out for state income taxes.

Your employer is not allowed to tell you what to put on this form. So if this is your first job and you are not sure how to fill this out, ask someone even before you apply for a job – you don't want to look completely inexperienced. (Perhaps make a note and tuck it into your wallet.)

Filing Income Tax Returns

The federal and state governments have a complex set of calculations that determine who must pay how much, in taxes. An over-simplified explanation looks like this:

When you make $20,000 per year, you must pay 5 percent of that in federal taxes and maybe another 5 percent in state taxes. This money is usually taken out of your paycheck by your employer before you ever see it, so you don't have to worry about saving it up throughout the year. Your employer sends the money to the Internal Revenue Service (IRS) and the state's Franchise Tax Board (if applicable – not all states collect income tax) under your name and Social Security number.

At the end of every year you are responsible for reporting your income (the money you were paid to work), the amount of taxes you already paid to the federal government, and, in some states, the money you've paid to the state government. This is referred to as "filing your income tax returns." You have until April 15 in the following year to file your returns for the previous year.

You can file your taxes with the help of a computer program such as TurboTax, through a tax preparation service such as H&R Block, or by hiring a certified public accountant (CPA). Part of the preparation process will be doing all the calculations that let you know if you have already paid all you owe, if you paid too much, or if you didn't pay enough. If you paid too much, you will get a tax refund. If you didn't pay enough (your employer didn't deduct enough) then you will have to send in a check for the amount owed before the filing deadline of April 15th.

Deductions/Write-Offs

The government allows you to deduct a number of items from your tax bill, known as either "deductions" or "write-offs." In most cases these are dollar amounts that you subtract, or deduct from your total yearly income, thus lowering your taxable income.

Some examples of deductions for individuals would be child-care expenses, a "renter's" credit (for those who rent homes or apartments), mortgage interest, and property taxes.

Some examples of deductions for businesses would be business expenses such as office supplies, building/real estate costs, computers, telephones, and property taxes.

Loopholes

This term is often confused with tax deductions. However there is a fine line between the two terms: A deduction is clearly defined, a loophole is not.

Merriam-webster.com (2014) defines a loophole as, "an error in the way a law, rule, or contract is written that makes it possible for some people to legally avoid obeying it."

My simplified, more personal version of that is this: A tax loophole is when you can use your own opinion to calculate a deduction because the law is not clearly defined.

The most notorious business loophole is the one where a business can move its main office out of the United State to avoid paying federal income taxes.

On a smaller, more personal scale, I offer this example:

You can deduct a certain percentage of your mortgage for a home business (based upon the square footage of the house) if you do over 50 percent of that business in one particular room (the office) of the house. This phrase allows you to calculate the percentage of that business, the square footage of the room in which you are doing business, and make your own determination of the deduction you will take.

Since these types of calculations are open to individual opinion, they are really considered a "gray area" in the tax law. Most tax accountants will advise you to stay on the conservative side of these types of calculations knowing that the IRS frowns upon anyone taking advantage of them.

To calculate on the high side, or take advantage of loopholes is considered bad business, bad faith, and in some cases, tax fraud and therefore, illegal. Stay away from any tax man who sells you on his services by saying he's really good because he knows how to "work around all the loopholes."

Bank Accounts

It's difficult and costly to cash a payroll check, or any check (gifts from grandma) for that matter if you don't have a bank account.

Beneficiaries

One thing to keep in mind as you set up your bank accounts, is who you want your money to go to if you don't live long enough to use it yourself. The person or persons you specify are referred to as your "beneficiaries." If you are married with kids, you might select your wife or kids, or both. If you are single, though, you might consider a close family member such as a sister or brother, or even a parent. Give this some thought as you are filling out the forms for these accounts.

Also keep in mind as your life's circumstances and status change, such as marriage or divorce, you should update your beneficiaries.

Checking Accounts

This type of account comes with a book of checks that you can use to pay bills or fill out at a store to buy things such as groceries, clothes, household goods, or anything else you want.

Many banks will give you a "debit" card to use for the same thing. Anytime money is deducted out of your account for purchases, it's called a "debit" by the bank. Thus, the reason it's called a "debit" card.

It's best to use checks or a debit card to make purchases rather than carry cash. It's easier to lose cash or have someone steal it. But you can put a "stop payment" on a check. (Refer to Page 72 for more information about "Stop Payments" and "Debit Cards.") That way you won't lose the money.

Before you open a checking account, ask the bank about the fees it charges and how to get a "free" or "no fee" account.

Some of the fees I've seen charged look like this:

- The bank has a minimum balance requirement. This means you must keep a certain amount of money (your balance) in the account, such as $500. If the balance goes below that, the bank charges you a fee.

- Some banks only allow so many ATM (automated teller machine) transactions per month. If you go over you might be charged $1 or $2 per extra transaction.
- Some banks charge for every ATM transaction.
- My bank only allows me to make five transfers of money between checking and savings per month. I get charged $25 for each one after that.

Many banks will offer a free account if your paycheck is deposited automatically by your employer. (That is called "automatic payroll deposit.") So be sure to ask your employer if the company does automatic payroll deposits and also whether the bank that it works with offers free checking for that service.

Overdraft

Anytime you spend more money than is available in your checking account, it's called being "overdrawn," or having an "overdraft." And yes, the bank will generally pay the holder of the check or approve debit card transactions even when you don't have enough money in your account to cover it. When this happens, the bank will charge you an overdraft fee of $35, or more. It will take that money out of your account, which overdraws the account even more.

For example, if you make a mistake in calculating how much money you think you have, even by 1 cent, and your account becomes overdrawn, you will then be charged a $35 overdraft fee. Now you're overdrawn $35.01.

It is your responsibility to keep track of your balance so that this doesn't happen. That means, you should "balance your account" every month. Do not try to keep track in your head. Refer to Pages 77 and 161 for information about Balancing Your Account.

> *Tip:* **Some banks will reverse overdraft fees if you contact them and put money in the account right away. The key here is to contact them in person to take care of this. Again, this is "sometimes" and "some" banks; don't count on it.**

Stop Payments

Anytime you write a check to pay for something, and you are not happy with the purchase or service you bought, you have the option of cancelling the payment on it. That is called "stopping payment" on that check.

To do so, you must first make sure that check hasn't been paid: If it has been paid, then it's too late – you cannot stop payment on it; ***if it hasn't, request a stop payment on that check right away.***

Some banks require you to go in and talk with a bank representative to request a stop payment, some allow you to call in, or if you bank online, you can check to see if the item has been paid and there might also be an option to do the stop payment at the same time.

All banks will charge a fee for the stop payment – be sure to ask what that is before you sign the paperwork. Also ask how long the stop payment is good for – some banks put a time limit on it.

Debit Cards

When you open a checking or savings account you will likely be issued a "debit" card. This card allows you to pay for things at stores and restaurants or take money out of your account at an ATM machine (watch for fees on these).

While the card looks, acts and feels like a credit card, it's a bit different in that you do not get a bill at the end of the month. Each time you use the debit card, the expense (aka, dollar amount) is immediately deducted directly from your checking or savings account.

Pros

Most businesses will accept these for payment because they are identified as either a Master Card or Visa debit card. Any place that accepts credit cards or cash, will accept a debit card. That means you don't have to carry around a lot of cash when you're out and about. When you use a debit card for every cent you spend, the transaction hits your bank account almost immediately, so you can always check your balance online and have a fairly accurate idea of how much money you have available.

Cons

Because this is a direct line to your checking or savings account, it can be dangerous for any online business you might do. Scam artists are developing more and more sites designed to steal your money. Many scam sites will tie you to a monthly payment schedule for which you never intended to sign up. If you give them your debit card for payment, you are going to have a very hard time cancelling that payment either through that company or your bank. Therefore, your bank account might get drained before you can fix the problem.

Bottom line, do not use your debit card for online purchases. Get a separate credit card with a low credit limit ($100 to $500) for those purchases.

How to Write a Check

The practice of writing checks to pay for products and merchandise has been around for several hundred years. These days you can look up how to write a check on the Internet. However, I've included the steps here to save you some time.

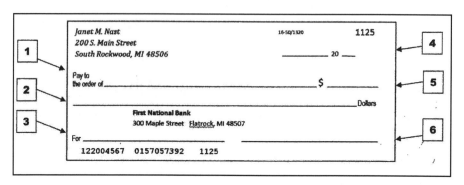

When writing a check, be sure to complete the following areas:

1. **Pay to the Order of:** Write the name of the person, or company, to whom you will give the check.
2. **Dollars:** Write the amount of the check in words, such as "twenty five and 97/100." After writing out the amount of the check, draw a line to the end. This prevents anyone from adding an additional amount after what you have written.
3. **For (or some say "Memo"):** This section is optional. You can use this area to remind yourself why you wrote the check or to record the account number of the bill you are paying.
4. **Date:** Write the current date.
5. **$:** Write the amount of the check in numbers, such as $25.97.
6. **Signature line:** Sign your name.

A correctly filled out check will look similar to this one.

```
Janet M. Nast                           16-50/1320              1125
200 S. Main Street
South Rockwood, MI 48506                  May 1    20 15

Pay to
the order of  Costco                                  $  25.97

  twenty five dollars and 97/100 ─────────────────────────── Dollars
              First National Bank
              300 Maple Street  Flatrock, MI 48507
For    coffee maker                         Janet M. Nast
    122004567    0157057392      1125
```

The numbers across the bottom of the check represent the following pieces of information about your checking account:

- The first group of numbers is referred to as the bank's "routing numbers." That's basically the location and branch of your bank.
- The middle group of numbers represents your checking account number.
- The last four to six numbers represent the check number; they should match the check number in the upper right-hand corner of the check.

Refer to Appendix B, on Page 161, to learn about "Balancing a Checkbook."

Shifting to the Business of Life

Savings Accounts

The main difference between a checking account and a savings account is that the bank will pay you interest on a savings account, but not a checking account (although some banks now pay interest on both types of accounts).

Generally speaking though, a savings account is where you put money that you don't want to spend for a long time. No checks are issued for a savings account because you probably won't use this type of account to pay bills or do your shopping. If your debit card (for checking) is connected to your savings account, that would only be for the purpose of transferring money between the two accounts. At point of sale, debit cards always take money from one account; in most cases, that is your checking account.

You do not have to have a savings account. That is optional.

Online Banking

Online banking allows you to manage your checking and savings account on the Internet as well as pay your bills online. This is not a requirement. It's your choice.

There are pros and cons to both scenarios. Personally, I don't care for it because it requires you to put a lot of personal information, along with your financial information (bank accounts, credit cards, etc) out on the "World Wide Web (WWW)," aka the Internet. So on one hand, it's my opinion (and possibly paranoia) any good hacker can get to that information if he or she wants to. But on the other hand, you can't beat it for the convenience.

Before you automatically sign up for online banking, do some research: Ask your bank what kind of protection you have if someone gets your checking account information and starts funneling money out of it. Some banks and many credit card companies keep track of your spending habits and will notice something out of the ordinary more quickly than you will. In that case, they call you to double check the odd transaction and then proceed to reverse things out if you say you didn't make that purchase.

If you're planning online transactions with your utility companies, your mortgage holder, or anyone else, find out what kind of protections those businesses provide. Most organizations are pretty secure these days.

Balancing Your Checking Account: On-Line vs. Paper

Most banks will send you a paper or electronic statement once a month that lists of every bit of money that came in to, or went out of, your account(s).

When you do all your banking (and other transactions) either online or with a debit card, you can probably get away with just checking your balance online occasionally to verify it. But I would still do a quick review of the paper (or electronic) version of your statement to check for any fees you might have been charged or had forgotten about.

However, if you use a combination of debit card, ATM, online payments and checks, then you really should "balance" your statement to your checking account every month. While your online transactions will come out of your account within 24 hours, the paper checks could sit around on someone's desk for weeks or months.

Part of balancing your account is making a list of the checks that haven't come through the account yet. That will give you a better idea of what you have available to spend.

If this second scenario sounds like something you need to do, refer to Appendix B, "Balancing a Checkbook," on Page 161 for steps on how to do so. Most banks will also teach you how to do this.

Budgeting

Budgeting means to look at how much money you bring home each month and decide (by doing some simple math) how much you can spend on various things. I strongly suggest you write this out in a notebook or in an electronic spread sheet each month.

Here is how you begin:

- In one column, write down your total monthly income.
- Below that, make a list of whom you owe money to.
- Next to each name, write down how much you need to pay them each month.
- Then simply subtract the amount you owe from the amount of money you are making and see what you have left.

Your budget file might look similar to the following example.

Description	Date	Amount				
Fred's 1st Paycheck	8/1/2014	$ 1,455.36				
Fred's 2nd Paycheck	8/16/2014	$ 1,456.72				
Totals		$ 2,912.08				

Name	Amt. Due	Date Due	Date Paid	Amt Paid	Check #
Rent	$ 800.00	8/1/2014	8/1/2014	$ 800.00	,10909
The Gas Co.	$ 25.30	8/19/2014	8/11/2014	$ 25.30	,10920
Electric	$ 56.00	8/21/2014	8/11/2014	$ 56.00	,10922
EnerBank	$ 269.46	8/18/2014	8/11/2014	$ 269.46	,10919
AT & T Cell Phone	$ 146.19	8/28/2014	8/21/2014	$ 146.19	,10928
AAA Car Ins.	$ 122.20	8/18/2014	8/18/2014	$ 122.20	auto debit
Ford Motor Cr. Co./USAA	$ 412.04	8/27/2014	8/21/2014	$ 412.04	,10923
Auto Trf to Savings	$ 100.00	8/18/2014	8/18/2018	$ 100.00	auto trf
Total In				$ 2,912.08	
Total Paid Out				$ 1,931.19	
What's left				$ 980.89	
Gas in Car					
Groceries					
Lunch Money					

You can see in the example that I've also included an "Auto Trf to Savings" of $100 a month just for emergencies that might come up such as a flat tire. If you find you can save more, then you should. In this case, that still leaves $980.89 for things like gas, groceries and lunch money.

It's a good idea to take this a step further by including numbers for those three items as well. It will help you to better determine if you have money left in your budget for other things, like going out to dinner, purchasing birthday gifts or taking a trip to Las Vegas.

In the case of a trip, you might want to save up for that by putting some money away in a separate savings account each month.

One more huge tip: Ideally, your monthly income should always be four times your rent so that you have enough money left over for all the expenses mentioned here and throughout the rest of this handbook. As you can see in the previous example, this individual might be living on mac and cheese for a while if any emergency expenses come up.

All of these suggestions are referred to as "budgeting." This process will help you avoid running out of money between paydays – also known as "living paycheck to paycheck" – and will help you sleep better at night.

Credit

Credit as defined by MiriamWebster.com, 2014:

- Money that a bank or business will allow a person to use and then pay back in the future
- A record of how well you have paid your bills in the past
- An amount of money that is added to an account

Credit Scores

This is a number that tells financial institutions, your employer (yes, your employer) and anyone else who needs to know, your credit worthiness. "Credit Worthiness" means this: If someone loans you money, how likely are you to pay it back and pay it back on time? Credit scores are also referred to as your FICO (Fair, Isaac &

Company) score since that is the company that developed it back in 1989.

Any company with whom you have set up a line of credit or from whom you have borrowed money will send your financial/payment history to the following three credit reporting agencies for the purpose of constantly monitoring your credit performance: Experian, Equifax and TransUnion. They collect and connect your information to you by the use of your Social Security number. (Refer to Page 19 to learn more about Social Security numbers.)

Credit scores range from 300 to 850. The higher the number, the better you look on paper and the more likely credit and loan companies will extend credit to you. The lower the number, the more untrustworthy you look to anyone – including an employer.

A company generally won't hire someone who looks like he or she has financial problems, whatever the reason.

Here are a few key points that explain what kind of information is used to determine your credit score, and how to keep that credit score on the high side:

Always pay your bills on time. That includes, but is not limited to, these types of bills:

- Cell phone company
- Apartment rentals
- Utilities (electricity, gas, water, phone lines)
- Credit cards
- Car loans
- Home loans

If you ever think you will be late on one of these payments, call the company affected and let it know. In many cases, the company will make a note on your account, and then won't report the late payment to the credit reporting agencies.

If you find that you cannot pay all of your bills for whatever reason (job loss, illness) then look into some sort of bill consolidation loan – ***don't just stop paying your bills.***

Consult a bankruptcy lawyer if that seems like your only option.

> <u>Note:</u> *Failing to pay your bills or declaring bankruptcy will ruin your credit incredibly fast. And both can stay on your credit report for up to seven (7) years.*

You are legally allowed to obtain a free copy of your personal credit report and credit scores once a year. I strongly suggest that you do this so you can spot and catch any errors or other problems, such as identity theft (Page 21), as soon as possible. As of 2015, two sites from which you can obtain such a report are:

> https://www.creditkarma.com/
> https://www.annualcreditreport.com/

Why are Credit Scores Important?

When you turn 18, one of the first things you might want to do is either get a cell phone account in your own name or buy your first car. However, if you have no credit history – and therefore, no credit score – no one will trust you to pay a phone bill or repay a car loan. For the same reason, it is also unlikely that you will be able to rent an apartment or get your electricity turned on if you do find a rental. That's why you should be concerned about establishing credit as well as maintaining a high credit score.

One other point to consider: The higher your credit score, the lower the interest rate you will be charged for loans. You can learn more about interest rates by looking at Page 91(for a general description), Page 94 (for Annual Percentage Rate (APR) description) and Page 102 for information on car loans.

How to Get Credit

First, get a job. (Refer to the section titled "Employment," on Page37, for details.)

Some of your employment history will appear on your credit report: Where you work, or have worked, and for how long.

It would be smart to stay ahead of the game by getting a job when you turn 16 (with your parents' permission, of course).

Don't drop out of school to work, though: Dropouts will be limited to minimum-wage jobs for most of their lives.

Also, you must work for a real company; not for Uncle Joe who's been paying you cash to help him deliver newspapers or mow the lawn. It needs to be a company that issues a paycheck and deducts taxes and Social Security.

Second, as soon as you've been at your job for at least six months, apply for a credit card.

Some credit cards are easier to get than others. If you have a bank account, apply at your bank first. Some stores might issue you credit such as the GAP, Victoria's Secret, Old Navy, or Macy's, but they charge higher interest on balances that you don't pay off each month.

Remember, since this is your first credit card, you will probably only get a spending limit (aka, credit limit) of $100 or $200. That's OK; it's a start.

> *<u>Tip:</u> Sears is almost impossible so don't bother with that retailer until you're over 35 and have had the same job for at least 15 years!*

Third, if you've ever borrowed money from your parents and paid it back within the time frame on which the two of you agreed, they might be able to help you to establish credit. Here's how:

A smart parent will look at things like your general trustworthiness, how much money you make and how you manage your money before deciding to help out. In other words, if you have good credit with the "bank of mom," she could do things like co-sign on a car loan for you, or co-sign on your first credit card account. I've done this for both of my kids to help them to establish credit and build a good credit score. After making payments on their car loans for at least two years, they had good credit and were able to refinance the balance of the loan in their own names.

Be aware, though, that if your parent co-signs and you miss a payment or stop paying altogether, that will reflect poorly not only on your credit, but also your parents' credit. Your parents' credit score could drop a few hundred points and really screw things up the next time they need a loan. So don't go into this kind of agreement lightly.

Credit Cards: How Do You Get One?

To get a credit card you have to fill out an application, similar to a job application. The application will ask for things like your name and address, employment history, and your Social Security number.

How They Work
When you fill out a credit application, you are essentially applying for "a line of credit" from a bank or retail store. This means that your bank, or the retailer's bank, has set aside a certain amount of money for your use any time you want. You spend it by using the credit card. So when you want to go out to eat or buy a new shirt and you don't have the cash, use the credit card. The bank (that issued the card) will see each transaction and give each store the money you spent.

But, here's the tricky part: ***The bank that gave the money in your name expects you to pay the money back.*** The bank will send you a reminder – otherwise known as a "bill" – each month for the amount you owe.

You can either pay it back all at once, or you can pay a little bit every month. The bill will show you how much you can pay each month, and it will also show you what it's going to cost you to carry that loan from one month to the next. That "cost" is called "interest." (Refer to the next section called "Interest," on Page 91, for more details.)

Here's an example of how it works:

I have a Visa card from Chase Bank. The bank has given me permission to spend up to $5,000. This is my "credit limit." I can take that Visa card to Macy's and use it to buy new shoes, dresses, and makeup for $2,000. Now I owe Chase Bank $2,000.

The bank will send me a bill to remind me of that fact and it expects me to send some money each month until I pay it all back. The bill will show that I have the option of paying $30 a month and will charge me 18 percent interest on the rest until I pay off the $2,000. So it's in my best interest to pay it off sooner rather than later. If I don't, I will quickly see how much 18 percent of a running balance can add up to.

What that means is that interest will be calculated on – and added to – whatever remaining balance is carried over to next month's bill. That is called "**compounded**" interest, which means it just keeps getting added or "compounded" onto the remaining balance each month until it's all paid back.

Most credit card bills will include a little chart that shows how much interest you will pay on a balance if you pay it off in say, two years as opposed to five years.

The lesson here is this:

While having credit cards can seem like a bad thing because of the compounded interest, they can be a good thing when you use them responsibly. When banks see that you have a high credit limit, but are only using a small fraction of that "available credit" on a regular basis, then you are being responsible, and therefore, are a good credit risk.

Thus your credit score may go higher. (Refer to Page 83 for more information about credit scores.)

Here are some examples of why you might want a credit card:

- **Emergencies:** You get a flat tire or your car breaks down unexpectedly.
- **Travel:** Carry a little bit of cash and use credit cards to pay for expensive (big-ticket) items such as hotels and rental cars.
- **You are trying to build credit,** so use your card to buy something small every three to four months, such as a new shirt, a set of towels, or seasonal items when they go on sale. When you pay that off, do it again.

Interest

Interest can be defined two ways:

First, it can be money that a bank gives you when you let it hold onto your money for any length of time. This means that your money is "earning interest." Two examples of where you can put your money to earn interest are:

- A savings account – Banks pay either monthly or quarterly interest on the balance you have at the time they pay. The more you have in there, and the longer it stays there, the more interest you earn.

- A Certificate of Deposit (CD) - This is basically a large amount of money that you let the bank hold onto for a period of time (such as $5000 for one year). For that period of time, it earns interest and you cannot touch it. If you do, you will be charged all sorts of fees and end up with less than you started with.

Second, it can be extra money you pay to the bank when you borrow money for items such as a car loan, a home loan or a credit card. (Refer to Page 88 for more information about credit cards.)

In the case of a credit card for example, you are paying **"compounded"** interest. This means the lending bank will start charging you interest the minute you use your card to pay for something. It looks like this: A typical interest rate is 18 percent. So let's say you charge $100 and you make a $20 payment. Then next month 18 percent ($14.40) is added to the $80 balance. Now you owe $94.40. If you pay another $20, you'll owe $74.40, plus 18 percent ($13.39) or $87.79. Yes this sucks, but that's the way it works.

In the example of buying a piece of furniture, you may be charged **"simple"** interest. Say you buy a sofa for $2,000 at an interest rate of 4 percent. That means that 4 percent is multiplied by 2,000 and the total - $80 – is added to your loan. The company will then take your new balance of $2,080 and divide it by, say, 12 months which means you'll be paying $173.33 per month till you pay it off.

Car loans and home loans work a little differently. But regardless, when you decide to purchase something, you should always look for the lowest interest rate possible. (Turn to Page 102 for information on interest rates for car loans.)

Cost of the Loan

This term refers to what a bank or lender is charging you for borrowing its money. Generally this cost will be charged via "interest rates". But some lenders will tack on other fees, such as administrative fees. Always ask about the cost of the loan no matter what kind of loan you are applying for (cars, appliances, homes). And read the fine print scattered throughout the loan papers: Many fees – referred to as "hidden fees" – will be listed there.

Fiscal Year vs. Calendar Year

A calendar year runs from January to December. Most people live their lives, work their jobs, pay off their loans and file their taxes all based upon the calendar year.

A fiscal year usually starts at the beginning of a quarter: January 1, April 1, July 1 or October 1. Some businesses that have higher sales in the fall and higher business expenses in the spring, might want their fiscal year to start on Oct 1. That way they have a better idea of what their income will be for the year, and can adjust their expenses to maintain their desired profit margins. Since many companies can file "fiscal" taxes, this can work to their advantage.

APR

This stands for "Annual Percentage Rate." This is the amount, or percentage of interest (including fees), that a bank will charge you for a loan in a year. For instance, if you get a one year loan for $1,000 and the APR is 7 percent, the amount of interest you will pay on that loan in that one year is $70. The lender will then take the total, $1070 and divide it by 12, for the twelve months in the year, thus, making your payments $89.17 per month. Keep in mind, though, that some banks and other lenders will also charge a monthly interest rate on top of that. As always, the higher your credit score, the lower your interest rate might be.

No Interest for 24 Months

After learning about interest and how much it can cost you, this seems like a great deal. Well, in some cases it can be. There are two ways this can work and you should understand them before you sign on the dotted line for this sort of deal.

Balance Transfers
First, on a credit card you might see the offer of "0 Percent Interest on Balance Transfers for 24 Months." They are saying that you can transfer a balance from another credit card (where you might be paying 28 percent interest), to this new one that won't charge you any interest…for 24 months. ***But what the fine print says is that the credit card company will charge you 4 percent of the balance amount you want to transfer and tack that on the minute you transfer.***

For example, you owe $1000 on another credit card (Bank of America Visa) and the bank charges you 26 percent interest per monthly. A four percent balance transfer fee to a Chase Master Card is quite a bit less.

Honestly, this is not a bad idea, especially if you can pay the balance off in 24 months. Even if you can't, the bank will just look at what you owe after 24 months (maybe only $400 now) and will start charging its normal interest rate on that ... which might be 18 percent or more. At least you were able to knock some of the balance down without getting charged 26 percent interest for two years.

24 Months Same as Cash (aka, Deferred Interest)

The second way zero percent interest can work is when you are financing something like furniture. When they say "0% interest for 24 months" they mean that if you pay off the balance of the loan in 24 months, they will not charge you interest.

So, on a $2,000 loan where they might normally charge 20 percent interest ($400), as long as you pay off the $2000 in 24 months, you won't have to pay that extra $400. But if month 25 comes up and you miscalculated and still owe another $20 – well now you have $400 added to your balance. This is known as "deferred interest." They only pushed out the interest amount ($400) for 24 months.

Again, this can be a great idea. Just do the math before you sign up for it: Make sure you can pay off the loan in the specified amount of time. If you can, then you are borrowing money for free, and that's a good thing!

Shifting to the Business of Life

Buying a Car/Vehicle

A lot of costs are not discussed up front when you buy a car. So be aware that the sticker price on a car is not the total price you will pay. The next few sections describe all possible expenses you should be aware of before you sign a purchase or lease agreement for a new vehicle.

By the way, all the information in these car/vehicle sections applies to cars, trucks, motorcycles, quads, motor homes and any other rolling vehicle you can think of. I have used the word "car" just to keep it simple.

The Sticker Price

When you buy a car from a car dealer, this is the price you see on the paper stuck to the window of the car. That paper will list all the accessories on the car (air conditioning, stereo, leather seats, cruise control, etc.) and their related costs totaled into one price at the bottom: The "sticker price."

Either way, the sticker price (from a dealer) will not include several items: The sales tax, the amount of interest on a loan (if you aren't paying cash for the car), the cost to register the car in the state (aka, the licensing fees) and any warranties the dealer may try to sell you.

Used Cars

Dealers sell used cars (at lower prices than new cars) and so do individual people (aka, private parties). When a dealer sells it, it will probably have a sticker price on the window and you will have to consider all those extra add-on fees I mentioned in the previous section about buying a new car. Ask the dealer about all those things before you sign on the dotted line.

When you buy a car from a private party it will usually be a used car (one that an individual has owned and used for a day, a week a year or many years). Then there is no sticker, but the seller will sometimes refer to the price of the car as the "sticker price." In that case, it probably *is* the total price of the car. But be sure to ask; otherwise you won't know until you go to pay for it. (For more information about purchasing or selling used cars, turn to Page 107 and Page 111 respectively.)

Car Insurance

This insurance pays for damage to you, your car, and someone else's car or property in the event you hit someone, aka, get in an accident. Almost every state requires you to have car insurance, and keep proof of said insurance along with your registration (see Page 110) in the car, if you plan on driving a car on public roads. (Private property, maybe not – but check with your local Department of Motor Vehicles to make sure).

It is important to know that car insurance only covers damage done to your car in an accident. It doesn't cover mechanical failure or wear and tear. This means you are responsible for all maintenance of your vehicle including: Windshield wiper replacements; tire replacements; oil changes; fluid leaks; any engine, transmission and drive train repair; and brake replacement or repair. (Your owner's manual will suggest appropriate times for periodic maintenance checks.) Anything that breaks just by virtue of being used or wearing out will not be covered by insurance. **Some dealers will offer extended warranties to cover some of these eventualities, but not insurance.** (Call the dealer and find out how to deal with warranty issues. Refer to Page 106 for more information on warranties.)

Dozens of insurance companies out there want to sell you insurance and they all will try to convince you that they have the best monthly "rates" or payment plans. Rates will be determined by the type and amount of coverage you ask for, the type and value of the car you want to insure, and your personal driving history.

Personal driving history will include length of time you've been driving, your age and how many tickets or accidents you've had.

Insurers may also ask how far you drive to work every day, and where you live. Cities with more traffic such as Los Angeles or New York, for instance, charge higher rates. And the more you drive, the more likely you are to get into an accident.

Some coverage issues you should consider:

- How much will the insurance pay for repairs if your car is damaged or someone else's car is damaged?
- How much will it pay for you or the other person's medical bills if either of you is hurt?
- How much will it pay if you damage someone's property – for instance if you hit a sign at a place of business or drive through the front of a building?
- If you let a friend drive your car and he or she gets in an accident, will it still cover all costs?
- What are the deductibles? This means the amount of cash you have to pay before the insurance coverage kicks in. (More information on deductibles can be found in the next section.)
- Does the company cover the cost of a rental vehicle while your car is being repaired?
- Will the company insist that you only use its repair shops? That is illegal in every state, so don't get insurance with any company that says this.
- Does it cover the cost of towing when you're in an accident, or for a breakdown (dead battery, out of gas, etc.)?
- Does it pay 100 percent for windshield repair? (This can happen when rocks get thrown up while you're driving on the highway.)

Since every insurance company will charge different dollar amounts for the same coverage, call around and compare pricing…and take notes.

Deductibles

When you are involved in an accident and need to file a claim with your insurance company, your deducible is the amount of money you have to pay for repairs or medical bills before the insurance company starts paying. This is something you need to seriously consider when you first sign up for auto insurance because it can affect your yearly insurance cost.

For instance, if you have a collision deductible of $250, you might pay $1500 for the whole year for your insurance. But if you ask for a higher deductible, such as $1,000, then your cost for the yearly policy could drop to $1,100. When you divide that into monthly payments, that $33 a month savings might make the difference in whether or not you eat lunch every day. Before you sign on the dotted line, consider these two things:

- How many accidents have you been involved in, in the last year?
- Do you have $1,000 to pay out if you get into an accident?

If you feel you are a safe driver, and the insurance company agrees, then you might want to consider having higher deductibles and putting that extra money in the bank.

Down Payments

This is the money you give to the car dealer or lender to bring down the price of the car. Some dealerships require a down payment, some don't. Some say they want a down payment because your credit score is low and they don't want to loan you the full amount for the car. (In that case they will also charge you a higher interest rate.) Some say it's company policy to have a 10 percent down payment on all cars that have to be financed. This really is up to the individual dealer so be prepared to pay a few thousand dollars up front when you buy a car.

Financing a Car Loan

You can choose to finance your car through the dealership or through a bank of your choice. I even put one car purchase of mine on a credit card. I later got a bank loan though because the credit card was charging 13 percent compounded interest (which was recalculated each month on the new balance), and the bank only charged a one-time interest rate of 5 percent on the total amount of the loan.

Interest Rates on Car Loans
This is what a bank will charge you for the privilege of letting you borrow money for a certain period of time. And always remember, the higher your credit score, the better chance you will be charged a lower interest rate.

The table on the following page shows an example of what payments could look like on a $20,000 car loan.

Sticker Price	$20,000
8% sales tax	$1,600
Sub-total	$21,600
Registration (varies from state to state)	$500
Extended 5-yr. warranty	$1,200
Sub-total	$23,300
Down Payment	$2,000
Sub-total (the loan "principle")	$21,300
Interest on the loan (15% over 5 years)	$9,103.53
Total cost of the loan	$30,403.53
Monthly pmts for 5 yrs (the "term" of the loan)	$506.73

As you can see above, the bank or car dealer will add up the total cost of the car by adding sales tax, licensing and warranty costs, then subtract your down payment. Your loan amount, referred to as the *"principle,"* is now $21,300. Each month (during the term of the loan) you make a payment, the interest will be recalculated on the new, lower principle amount.

This calculation is often referred to as "loan amortization." In order to see exactly how this works, take a look at the complete amortization chart for this car loan in Appendix A on Page 157.

You will be faced with a similar calculation anytime you buy any high-priced (aka, "big ticket") item such as a boat or house.

Purchase vs. Lease

Purchasing a car means that when you finish making all the payments after three to five years, you own the car and the bank sends you the "pink slip" (the certificate of title for the car – see Page 109 for more information about pink slips).

Leasing means that you are essentially renting the car for a specified number of years. All the interest and warranties work basically the same way. But the amount you pay is calculated differently. For instance, if the sticker is $20,000, the lender might just calculate the "loan" on $10,000 for three years. The advantage is that your payments will be lower. You cannot easily get out of a lease agreement, though, and if you try, there could be fees and penalties.

Many people choose this route because they can get lower payments. But, you must have very good credit (some banks require you to be a homeowner) to qualify for a lease. At the end of the lease you may want to purchase the vehicle by paying off the balance you haven't yet paid. You could also choose to lease a new vehicle or turn in the car, walk away and owe nothing.

Again, the advantage to leasing is that you have a lower amount to finance, so your payments can be quite low. I don't recommend this route for buying a car because you will be paying on it for the length of the lease (maybe four years) and then another three to five years on that remaining balance, aka the "balloon" payment. So this turns out to be a seven to nine year payment plan with a lot of interest paid over those years.

Another possible trouble spot when you lease a car is that there may be a limit to the number of miles you are allowed to drive during the lease period. Some are 12,000 miles a year, some are more. If you go over the number of miles by the end of the lease, and you choose to turn the car back in (rather than buy it) you will have to pay the dealer so much per mile for every mile over that limit.

Read the lease; it will specify the number of miles and the cost per mile beyond that limit. If you decide to buy the car at the end of the lease, do it a few months before the lease is up then you're less likely to exceed the permissible miles.

You'll want to discuss this with the dealer because they all calculate lease agreements differently. But more importantly, talk to someone you trust about finances and see if this is a good or bad option for you.

Contracts/Purchase/Lease Agreements

Regardless of what you decide to do: Read all the contracts, warranties and agreements before you sign anything!

If you don't like something in any of these documents after you sign them, you are SOL (shit out of luck)! You can't "un-ring that bell" or un-sign these documents. They are all legal and binding; you can be taken to court, sent to collections, or have the car repossessed (taken back) by the dealer or bank if you decide to get mad and stop making payments. What's more, your credit score will go down the tubes.

So, if you are nervous or overwhelmed about buying your first car and you have no idea what any of these documents really mean, take someone with you who has some experience. And don't believe anyone who tells you, "You don't have to read it. It's all standard stuff, so you can just sign – it's no big deal." If the dealer says this, it's probably a lie, he's trying to hide something, or he's in a really big hurry to move on to the next deal. If your friend says this before reading the documents, then he or she probably doesn't know any better.

Read everything before you sign it – no matter how long it takes!

By the way , if the seller tries to rush you, you can either walk away, or ask for a blank copy to take home and read overnight. A lot of people read contracts so there is no reason to feel embarrassed. And, since you can walk away, it means that that individual could lose the sale – and his or her commission. You can bet he or she doesn't want that to happen. So, again,

Read everything before you sign it – no matter how long it takes!

Vehicle Warranties

Warranties are basically an "insurance" that a car dealer will either include in the cost of the vehicle or sell to you when you buy a car. A warranty usually covers all mechanical parts of your car that might break within a specified amount of time. Among the items typically included:

- Any faulty parts inside the car such as door locks, windows, radio, power seats, heated seats, etc.
- Fluid leaks such as oil or transmission fluid
- Any engine, transmission and drive train issues
- Some dealers might include free tune-ups (you need to ask if that's included, and what it covers)

Things you should maintain yourself because of use or normal wear and tear probably will not be covered, but it never hurts to ask. Turn to the section about, "Personal Vehicle Maintenance," on Page 108 to see a list.

When you buy a brand-new car from a dealer (the only way the average person can buy a brand-new car) in most cases you will receive a good warranty on the car. Since selling cars has become so competitive, you can get things like 10-year, "bumper to bumper" warranties that even include "free oil changes for as long as you own the car." Ask the dealer.

You might also get a warranty when you buy a used, or "pre-owned," car from a dealer. It's trendy for dealers to label their cars as "Certified Pre-Owned." In that case, you will probably get a good warranty. Ask the dealer. If there is no warranty for whatever reason, take a friend with you who knows what to look for with regard to oil, worn-out hoses, and wear and tear on most mechanical parts under the hood and under the car. Most importantly, test drive the car.

When you buy a used car from an individual (or private party, someone whom you've probably never met before) you won't get a warranty. The risk you take in buying a used car is that the previous owner never took care of it, and the engine could blow up on you within a week of driving it away. Take a friend with you who knows what to look for or ask the seller if you can take the car to a mechanic for an assessment.

Lastly, and most importantly, test drive the car.

Personal Vehicle Maintenance

Although you get insurance and a warranty, there are still many things for which you are responsible in order to keep your car running safely. If you want to save money, learn how to do the things listed below on your own. Otherwise, find a reliable, trustworthy mechanic.

Most of these items and tasks should be done as part of what they call a "tune-up" on your car and should be done on a regular basis such as every four to six months. Your vehicle's user manual will tell you when some of these things should be done. Common sense will dictate other things such as windshield washer refills, and tire replacement. All you need to do is look.

Standard maintenance should include, but is not limited to:

- Windshield wiper replacements
- Windshield washer fluid refills
- Tire repairs or replacements
- Oil changes
- Spark plug and wire changes
- Checking and replacing all belts along with checking and resetting engine timing
- Checking for cracks on all hoses and seals, and replacing when worn

Pink Slip

This is your "receipt" and proof of ownership for your car. All vehicles have these and all vehicles have to be registered with the Department of Motor Vehicles in your state.

Before you pay off your car, the bank (or whoever loaned you the money for the car) holds onto this document and it lists the lender's name as the "legal" owner. Once you've paid off the loan, the lender (or bank) transfers ownership to you by filling out and signing the "transfer of ownership" information on the back of the pink slip (the actual color may vary), which then gets sent to the Department of Motor Vehicles (DMV), The DMV puts its stamp of approval on it and sends the revised pink slip to you.

You have to complete the same process when you buy a used vehicle from someone. The seller should have the pink slip handy when you pay for the car. He or she must fill out the transfer information on the back of that document and hand it over to you. You must then take it to the DMV to get the change recorded. There will probably be a transfer fee, too. When done, you should file this document in a safe place. That way you have it handy in case you decide to sell the car.

Refer to page 117 for more information and to see an example of the back of a California pink slip.

Registration at the DMV

All vehicles are registered with the state's Department of Motor Vehicles (DMV). Different states may call this office by another name, but they all serve the same purpose: They keep track of all things on wheels and those of us who move them around.

If you want to drive a car, it must be registered at the DMV (for a fee that varies from state to state) and the DMV will issue a license plate for it. This license and registration must be paid (renewed) on the same date every year. You will receive new stickers (tags) and a registration card each year when you renew.

You must put the tags on your license plate in the little squares designated for them.

You need to have the registration card, along with proof of insurance, with you whenever you drive the car. Some people put both documents in their glove box; some people carry them in their wallet or purse. It really doesn't matter where you keep these cards but if you get stopped by a police officer, you'd better be able to show both to the officer when he or she asks for them.

Selling a Car/Vehicle

When you sell a car for any reason, you have two choices; sell it to a dealer or sell it to a private party. Before you do either, you should look up the "Blue Book" value to make sure you know what your car is worth and how much you can ask for it.

Kelley Blue Book

When printed in hard copy, the Kelley Blue Book is actually dark blue. (The original book was written by Les Kelley, who started the Kelley Car Company in 1918.) These days the same information is available on the KBB.com website as well as a smart phone app. Look it up on the Internet or your app store.

The information contained within is all about the value of used cars, aka, the "Blue Book value." This value is determined, in part, by the following types of information:

- Make, model and year of the car
- How many miles are on the car's odometer
- Any mechanical features such as engine size, four-wheel drive or two-wheel drive, type of transmission (standard/shift or automatic), etc.
- Accessories such as type of stereo, CD player, sunroof, etc.
- Condition of the interior and exterior

The online site will usually display drop-down lists of options from which you can choose as soon as you select the make, model and year.

The results will usually include two different values:

- The wholesale/dealer value

This is what a dealer will pay another dealer for the car. As a private party, you will receive much less. That is because once the dealer buys the vehicle from you, they will try to resell it for a profit. If that doesn't work, the dealer will "wholesale it" to another dealer. Either way, the dealer has to make money on it.

- The personal retail value

This represents a fair value and the price you can ask when selling your car to another person.

Sell/Trade to Dealer

This is called, "trading your old car in" for a new car. You may want to do this when buying a new car from the same dealer just to save time. The advantage is that you can do both transactions at the same time, in the same place, with the same person.

If you still have an outstanding loan on your old car, trading it in is also easier because the dealer will be able to pay off your old loan and transfer pink slips for you through the Department of Motor Vehicles.

In the case where you owe more on the old car loan than what the car is worth, a trade-in is your best option. Owing more than the car is worth is referred to as being *"upside down"* on the loan. Say you owe $20,000 on the loan, but the Blue Book value is only $17,000. You are "upside down" by $3,000. The dealer would be more than happy to tack that onto the price of your new $25,000 car and make you a loan of $28,000. This is a deal you probably cannot make on your own, so you would have to work with a dealer.

On the other side of the coin, you might owe less on the loan, or nothing, compared to the value of the car. This means that you have *"equity"* in your car. For instance, if you owe $2,000 on the loan, but the car value is $15,000, then you have $13,000 equity in your car.

The disadvantage of trading your car in with a dealer (in that situation) is that you will probably not get the full value for your car in the trade: The dealer knows the Blue Book value, and will probably pay you less than half that price. Yes, that dollar amount would then be subtracted from the price of the car you want to buy (called a "down payment" or "cash down"). However if you sell the car yourself, you will more likely get the full Blue Book value, and, in turn, you will have more cash to either put in your pocket, put down on the new car, or both.

Sell It Yourself

This option does take some time and effort on your part, but financially, you will come out ahead.

If you still have a loan on the car, this might be trickier because you do not have the pink slip in your hands; the bank does. The bank won't send it to you until you pay off the loan. If the buyer of your car is willing to wait, then go for it. If the buyer won't wait, then your choices are to find another buyer or work with a dealership.

Here are the steps involved in the process of selling your own car:

First, decide on a selling price. Begin by looking up the Blue Book value on your vehicle. Then check the local online ads for the same car to see what others are asking. If you are asking a lot more than other folks, you might have a hard time selling it.

When you decide on a price, be sure to ask for just a little more (say a few hundred dollars) so you have some room to negotiate down to the price you really want.

Next, decide where you want to show the car. Do you want people to come to your house to look at it, or somewhere else such as a public parking lot at the grocery store? Ask yourself if you want perfect strangers coming to your house and knowing where you live if something doesn't go as planned. If not, pick a place and know how to direct people to that location when they call about your car.

Third, you need to place "for sale" ads for this car. There are many online options, such as Craigslist and Auto Trader, as well as local newspapers. Here is what you should include in your ad:

- The asking price
- The year, make and model
- Pictures – one from each of the four sides
- Features/accessories (leather upholstry, heated seats, six CD changer, Bose speakers)
- Any special options you might have added (new tires, chrome wheels, new paint, CB radio or car cover)
- Specify cash only, or credit cards if you can take them. People have been known to write bad checks or even forge cashier's checks from the bank, so don't take them.
- Add a phone number or email where people can reach you for information.

Safety Issues

Regardless of where you choose to meet potential buyers, do so only in the daytime and in a place with a lot of other people around.

In most cases, when people come to buy a used car from a private party, they bring a friend to assure their own safety. You need to consider your safety too, so consider having a big, strong friend with you for these meetings.

The buyer will want to test drive your car, so make sure he or she has insurance and a driver's license. You or your friend (or both) should ride along. None of this is a "legal" issue, just a safety issue for all parties involved.

The Sale Process

Once you agree on a price, you need to write out a "bill of sale, aka, a receipt. It can be written on any piece of paper by hand or you can type out most of it ahead of time with areas in which you can fill in the pertinent information once you have it. It should include the following information:

- Your name and phone number
- The year, make and model of the vehicle being sold
- The Vehicle Identification Number (VIN) of the vehicle being sold
- The buyer's name and phone number
- The price
- The date and time
- The words, "This sale is final and you agree to the purchase of this vehicle as is, with no implied warranty." (This is so no one can come back and say that you have to replace or fix anything that goes wrong with the vehicle after he or she drives it away.)
- Both of you must sign and date this document.

Cash should trade hands at this point. ***Do not*** sign over the pink slip or hand over the keys until this critical step is done. Then secure the cash (in your wallet, other car, purse, vault) and continue with this next step.

Transferring Pink Slips

In the case of a cash transaction where you don't have a loan on the car, you will have the pink slip. Turn it over and read the instructions on the back:

- Fill it out as directed, make copies of the front and back if you can

(use a smart phone camera or a copier), give one half to the buyer and keep the other half.
- Take your half to the Department of Motor Vehicles.
- Then immediately call your insurance company and cancel the insurance on this car.

In the case where you have to pay off the loan on the car with the sale, you should call the bank ahead of time and get instructions on how to handle this situation. Your buyer will have to wait for the pink slip from your bank. When the transaction is complete, again, call your insurance company immediately to cancel the insurance on this car.

Shown here is an example of the back of a California pink slip. *(Yes, we all make mistakes, as you can see here.)*

Marriage

As an adult you need to realize that marriage is a legally binding, financial, business arrangement. You will be cohabitating, which means signing contracts together for either an apartment or a house. You might be getting joint bank accounts and joint credit cards. All these tasks involve legal and binding contracts or leases. Neither one of you can get out of any such agreement without the other's cooperation.

That said, it is a really good idea for you and your other half to have some serious discussions about finances and make sure that you both agree on how household finances are to be handled. This discussion should cover decisions about paying bills, how much of your combined income is "disposable," (aka, spending money), how much should be saved and for what.

You should also discuss whether you want to have kids, if you want to buy a house, and when to retire. This is not a complete list of things you should discuss with any potential spouse, but it should get you headed in the right direction. If you and your spouse-to-be don't agree on these main topics, you should seriously consider not marrying that person.

When you have decided to get married, there are a few other things you must do: Some are legally required, some are not. Read on.

Prenuptial Agreement

This is a legal document that you or your spouse-to-be (or both) might want to write up that contains information about your finances and possessions and how they would be divided between the two of you in the event of a divorce. It is *not* legally required. However, there is one basic phrase you should consider when debating whether or not to create a "prenup": Community property.

Imagine this scenario: You are rich and your fiancé is dirt poor. In a community property state, such as California, the minute you sign that marriage license and file it with the city, everything you own becomes "community property." As in, each of you now owns half of that. Therefore that dirt-poor person takes half with him or her if you divorce.

So before you get married, apply that general train of thought to things you might own and value very highly: Your favorite china, your antique furniture collection, a restored '57 Chevy. These could all possibly be considered "community property" after the wedding.

If you acquired them through a purchase after you get married, they are definitely community property and the fight could get pretty ugly if you were to divorce. Luckily, inherited property is not community property.

While a prenup is not required, it should be considered.

Marriage License

It *is* a legal requirement that you have a license to get married. Depending upon the city or state, you can fill out an application for a marriage license in one of these places: Local city or county administration office, county clerk's office, or city hall. You will need one or two forms of identification such as a driver's license and/or a birth certificate. Call ahead and ask: Every city, state and country (if you choose to be married in another country) is different.

Oh, and these are not free. The last time I checked in the state of Nevada in 2003, it was $65. I believe in most states the cost is still under $100.

The Wedding

A big wedding is *not* required to get married. You can do a simple ceremony at city hall. A "justice of the peace" is typically available to do this for a small fee. (Again, call ahead to find out and to schedule the ceremony.)

There are plenty of wedding options other than using a justice of the peace. Whatever you decide to do, you must decide who is going to pay for what. Traditionally, the bride's family pays for the wedding, the groom's family pays for the rehearsal dinner (the dinner you provide for the wedding party after all of you rehearse the ceremony), and the groom pays for the bride's ring and the honeymoon. The bride pays for the groom's ring.

None of this is law, it's just tradition. In today's world, many couples are paying for their own wedding and parents often pitch in to help. Do what works best for you and your spouse-to-be.

Changing Names

It is traditional that the bride takes on the husband's last name (aka "surname") after the wedding. Another option is that the bride keeps her surname and hyphenates it with her husband's surname. Again, this is *not* law, just tradition, so do what's best for the two of you.

If you plan to change your name, these are the documents that you will need to file, with the appropriate offices:

Social Security Card

You must have your name changed on your Social Security card before you change it on other documents. This affects all your taxes, medical insurance, life insurance, retirement accounts and Social Security income when you retire: It's all connected.

If you are changing your name you must bring your marriage license and driver's license to your local Social Security office where you can fill out an application, show required identification and submit your completed paperwork. Your new card with your new name (same number) will arrive in the mail a few weeks later.

Driver's License

You must apply for another license in your new name. When you receive your new social Security Card, bring that along with a copy of the marriage license and current driver's license to the Department of Motor Vehicles, fill out and submit an application. Your new license with your new name (same number) will arrive in the mail a few weeks later.

Income Tax Filing Options

Once married you can no longer file taxes as "single." You can use either "married, filing jointly," or "married, filing separately." As far as which is better or worse, contact a tax professional to find out for sure.

Housing

Whether you are moving out by yourself for the first time, or moving in with a friend or new spouse, you need to know quite a few things before making that big move. Before you decide, take some time to compare the costs, prep work and supplies needed involved in renting an apartment vs. a house, and buying vs. renting.

Costs

Rent/Mortgage

The rule of thumb (regarding what you can afford for rent or a mortgage) is that your salary should be four times the amount of your rent or mortgage payment. For example, if your rent is going to be $1,000 per month, you should have a monthly salary of $4,000 after taxes (and all other deductions) are taken out. This allows you enough money to pay for monthly utility bills, car and gas, renter's insurance, food, yard and pool maintenance if applicable, and any entertainment such as going out to dinner or to the movies once in a while. These things add up much faster than you might think.

If you do the calculation and realize that your monthly salary is three times ($3,000) or two times ($2,000) your expected rent payment ($1,000), you should seriously consider a finding a roommate with whom you can split the rent. If not, you will be starving and losing a lot of weight really fast. It's up to you if that's a good or bad thing.

Moving Expenses

There are all kinds of expenses related to moving and then living on your own. Details of those are discussed throughout the next few sections. However, here is a short list of expenses to be aware of:

- Truck rental and gas for said truck when moving
- Security deposit on the rental truck
- Boxes and other packing materials
- Security deposits for your new home
  All landlords calculate this differently: Ask before making the commitment.

- Deposits to have utilities turned on (see Pages 127 and 132 for more information about utilities)

Ongoing Living Expenses
- Monthly rent/mortgage
- Renter's (Page 135) or homeowner's insurance (Page151)
- All monthly utility costs (Page 127)
- Groceries
- Other household supplies such as toilet paper and paper towels, soap, laundry detergent, etc.

- Quarters for doing laundry if you don't have your own washer and dryer
- Car Payment
- Car Insurance
- Gas for your car
- Cell phone (Page 35)
- Internet/Wi-Fi
- Savings (Page 76)
- Entertainment such as lunches or dinners out, movies, going out with friends

Utilities

Utilities include:

- Gas
- Electric (in some cities it could be "gas and electric")
- Telephone (if you would like a land line vs. relying solely on your cell phone)
- TV
- Water and trash service

There are two ways to find out what your monthly utilities might cost you:

First, if you are renting ask your landlord.

Second, if he/she doesn't know, or if you are purchasing a house, call the actual utility companies and ask what the last six months of charges were for that property.

The most important thing to know about utilities is that if you don't have any credit history or you have never had utility accounts in the city to which you are moving, you will probably have to pay a deposit for service. Call and ask each utility company to find out for sure. In that case, be sure to ask for how long the company will keep that deposit, and how you can get it back when that time is up.

Preparing to Move

Some tasks that need to be completed when preparing to move are:

- Give thirty days' notice to vacate
- Collect boxes and packing materials
- Pack all your belongings
- Get all your utilities turned on/off
- Submit a change of address to the local U.S. Post Office.
- Arrange to transport your belongings from one place to the next

30 Days' Notice to Vacate

When you rent month-to-month, most rental agreements contain a requirement to give the landlord (the person to whom you pay rent), a written thirty-day notice to vacate when you decide to move. That means if you want to move out on December 1st, you need to make sure that your landlord has a piece of paper in his or her hands on November 1st announcing that you are moving out on December 1st. It needs to contain your name, address (apartment number if you're in an apartment) and your signature.

To be safe, you should count the days in the month to make sure that between November and December there are thirty days. I once gave notice on Feb 1st that I was going to leave on March 1st and then ended up by having to pay rent for March too. I was told it was because there was only twenty-eight days in the month of February, therefore, I had not given thirty days' notice. (Yes, I also had to pay rent on my new apartment on the first of March.)

Also, in addition to mailing a copy of your thirty-day notice to the landlord at least two weeks before the thirty days begin (to allow for any delays in mail delivery), you might want to hand deliver another copy. If hand delivery is not possible (your landlord lives in another state), then I would strongly suggest some sort of registered mail for proof of delivery. Go to your local U.S. Post Office to learn about these options.

Exceptions: Military
There are exceptions for breaking rental leases and agreements such as an unexpected transfer or deployment when you are in the military. Ask the landlord before you sign the lease. It would also be a good idea to get this type of information in writing.

Exceptions: Other
There might be other exceptions for breaking rental leases and agreements. If you are concerned about that, ask the landlord before you sign anything and make sure you get any exceptions in writing.

Collecting Boxes and Packing Materials
There are a few ways you can gather packing boxes:

- You can ask all your friends and relatives to bring boxes home from their place of employment.
- You can collect them from grocery stores or other retail stores such as Home Depot or Hobby Lobby (ask an employee or go behind the store to the dumpster area). If you talk to the managers of these stores a month or two ahead of time, he or she might even agree to set aside boxes for you.

- You can go buy them from stores such as U-Haul or Lowes.

Packing materials also includes packing tape to seal the tops and bottoms of the boxes (yes, you should always reinforce the bottoms), a tape gun, as well as materials with which to wrap fragile things such as glasses, dishes, lamps or pictures in frames.

While you will have to buy the packing tape, you might be able to borrow a tape gun and use newspapers as packing materials. If you don't read the newspaper yourself, you can collect them from your neighbors after they're done reading them. By the way, don't use masking tape to save money – it's usually not strong enough to hold the contents of a packed box and you really won't be happy if the bottom of a box breaks open while it's being moved.

Packing Your Belongings

In order to make your move as quick, smooth and painless as possible (especially for the people who are helping you), it's a good idea to come up with a system for labeling your boxes. Here are a few suggestions:

Create one or two boxes with the label "First Day." This box should contain essential items needed for the first hour or day in your new home. You might even go so far as to include a room name on each one, such as:

Bathroom, which would include:

- Toilet paper
- Bath and face towels
- Toothbrushes and toothpaste
- Deodorant

- Soap, shampoo, shower gel (whatever you use in the shower)
- A change of clothes and underwear

Kitchen, which would include:

- Light bulbs
- Cups, dishes, silverware
- Paper towels or kitchen towels
- Food: At least one day's worth of meals
- Pots and pans in which to cook

Bedroom, which would include:

- Sheets, pillows and blankets
- All remotes for the TV/stereo/game consoles (these always get lost)

Label the remainder of your boxes using one of these four methods:

- **Put a number and a room name on each box.**
  Then keep a written list (on paper, not on a computer just in case the electricity doesn't go on until the second day after you move in) with all numbers and the contents of each box next to the number. The room name will help you remember where to put each box in your new home without having to just read the contents to figure it out.

- **Or - You could just label all your boxes with their contents** and then, as you are moving them, try to figure out which room they go in based upon that information.

- **Or - I've seen some folks not bother with contents and just put room names on each box.** That's always fun when you are trying to find the remotes in either the "living room" or "bedroom" boxes. Half the time they're in the "bathroom" box because everyone knows that that's where the toilet paper is and you know you'll open that box first.

- **Or - Lastly, you could put room names and contents on each box.**

Regardless of how you choose to label your boxes, just do something so that you and any helpers you have don't have to stop every five minutes and ask, "Where does this go?"

My last suggestion: Put everything in a box of some sort, even the "small stuff" that you think will just "go in the car." Unless you are moving by yourself, no one wants to carry your basket of dirty laundry, dirty dishes, or wet towels and toothbrush because it can, *"just fit in the car."* That's just nasty *and* mean.

Getting Utilities Turned On/Off

- Do this task at least sixty days before you move: Either ask your new landlord for phone numbers for all the utilities, or get on the Internet and look them up.
- Do not assume you can ask for utilities to be turned on or off (when you leave your previous home) in fewer than thirty days.
- Do not assume your new landlord will volunteer all this information: Ask!

   Note: See Page 127 for more information about utilities.

When you finally get into your new home, you need to learn where all the shut-off valves, and connections or breakers for water, gas, and electricity are located in the building. If something goes wrong with any of these you can call your landlord, or the utility company. But during evening or weekend hours, they might be hard to contact. So you should know this for your own safety.

Submitting "Change of Address"

The purpose of doing this is to make sure all your mail gets forwarded to you at your new home.

U.S. Post Office

An official "Change of Address" form can be picked up at any U.S. Post Office. It's a good idea to pick it up forty-five to sixty days before your move. The postal service prefers that you submit the completed form at least thirty days before you move. This gives it time to update all records.

Employer

Be sure to let your employer know your new address so they can assist with address changes on your insurance and retirement accounts, for example.

Bills/Creditors

Besides submitting this information to the Post Office, you should also fill out the individual change of address information for all your credit cards and any other loans you might have. This ensures that you will continue to receive your bills on time and thus, avoid any late payments and charges.

Current Landlord

In the case of moving from one apartment to another, you should also give your new address to your current landlord when you give your thirty-day notice to vacate (Page 128). That way your landlord can send you any refunds of security deposits (Pages 126 and 136).

Arrange to Transport Your Belongings
Even if you only have one box of clothes with a few kitchen and bath items, you need to find a way to move those boxes. Whether it be the trunk of your car, a friend's truck, or a moving van, plan ahead.

If you're relying on friends, no doubt you want to keep them as friends, so be considerate of their time, and give at least one month's notice…but two would be nicer. If you're renting a moving van, thirty days will usually suffice. But keep in mind that summertime is the busiest moving time of the year because of school schedules, so forty-five to sixty days notice would be better.

Be realistic when figuring out how big a truck you need. A few boxes and a bed and dresser might require a 10-foot-by-six-foot trailer. Furniture for a fully furnished two bedroom house might require a twenty-four-foot truck. Take a good guess and call ahead for pricing and the length of time you can keep the truck.

Moving is hard work and depending upon how much stuff you have and how many friends you have, the move itself could take three hours or twelve hours. If this all seems overwhelming, there is also the option of hiring a moving company. That of course, will cost you quite a bit more because you are now paying the salary of folks moving your boxes from your home to the truck, and then into the new home. Again, make that determination and that call for help at least thirty days before your scheduled move.

Renting an Apartment

When you decide to move into your own apartment, the first thing you must do is create a monthly budget to see what you can afford to do. Refer to Page 79 to learn how to create a budget, and Page 126 for a list of ongoing living expenses.

Renter's Insurance

This insurance will cover the cost of anything in your home that might get stolen or damaged by a guest or by a disaster such as flooding or a fire.

Many companies sell insurance, so be sure to get a couple of quotes and make sure you understand how much the policies cover (in dollars) and in what situations they cover damage or theft. Some will not cover flood damage for instance if you left the water running in the sink when you left the apartment. Some will not pay you the replacement cost of your fifteen-year-old hand-me-down sofa on which your friend started a small fire when drunk. The sofa might only be worth $25 in reality, but it will cost you $500 to get a new one: Will the insurance company pay you $25 or $500?

Bottom line, it's better to pay for renter's insurance rather than suffer the consequences if something is stolen or damaged. Just be sure to ask questions.

Rental/Lease Agreements

You can rent an apartment or house either "month-to-month" with no long-term commitment, or with a six month to one-year lease. Regardless of which way you do this, you will still be required to sign some sort of rental agreement. ***Read this document!*** Find out:

- Are deposits required (cleaning or pet or "security") and how much?
- Do you get your deposits back when you move out, and why or why not?
- What is the requirement for giving notice when you want to move (notice to vacate): Is it thirty days or sixty days?
- How many people can live in this apartment with you?
- What are the parking rules and regulations?
- Can you have pets (what kind and how many)?
- Are you required to obtain renter's insurance?
- What type of amenities or utilities are included in the rent such as use of laundry facilities, a pool, tennis courts, cost of water, trash, Internet/Wi-Fi, cable TV, etc.?

- Do you need separate keys or door codes to access any of the facilities?
- Is there a charge for lost keys? If so, what is it?

Roommates

In order to save on rent, you might want to consider sharing your home with friends, aka "roommates." That way you can split the rent by the number of tenants.

The most important thing you should do in a roommate situation is to make sure everyone's names and signatures are included on the rental agreement. This ensures that all parties involved have made the commitment to be accountable for the rent as well as any terms included in the agreement, such as the condition of the home.

Here are a few things that should be discussed and agreed upon amongst roommates:

- Who will sleep where?
- What do everyone's work, school and sleep schedules look like? This will help everyone to be aware of when quiet time is needed.
- What will the guidelines be regarding visitors? This discussion might include when visitors are welcome based upon work, school and homework schedules. Talk about evenings, weekends and overnight stays. And while it should be understood that each person is responsible for the behavior of their visitors, it is worth talking about up front.
- How will housework be split up? This might include discussions about keeping the common areas of the house clean such as the living room, bathroom and kitchen. In regards to the kitchen you

should discuss meal preparation as well as the subsequent clean up.
- How will you handle grocery shopping? Will you share things such as milk, eggs and cereal? This discussion might include where each persons' groceries are to be stored.
- How do you all feel about sharing personal items such as dishes, glasses, towels, silverware, pots and pans, toilet paper, soap, shampoo, laundry detergent, clothes, etc.?

These are just a few topics you should discuss with potential roommates. To learn more about the roommate experience, talk with your parents or other friends.

Month-to-Month vs. Lease

"Month-to-month" means that any time you feel like it, you can give your landlord (the person to whom you pay the rent) a thirty day's notice to vacate, and then move out anytime in that thirty day time frame. (See Page 128 for more information about giving notice.)

When you sign a "lease" for a specified amount of time (six months or one year is standard) you are agreeing to pay rent for that exact amount of time. While you could move out in the third month of a six month lease, you are legally responsible for paying the rent for the entire six months whether you live there or not. And it doesn't matter if you give thirty days' notice to vacate in that third month; you still must pay rent for the remaining months left on the lease.

That said, there are a couple exceptions to this rule; turn to Page 129 to learn about those.

Renting a House

This works pretty much the same as renting an apartment with regard to contracts, renter's insurance and notices to vacate. Refer to those sections for information on those topics.

There are a few other issues and costs you should consider when renting a house though. For easy reference, I've copied the apartment list here, and right below that are other things to consider when renting a house.

- Are deposits required (cleaning or pet or "security") and how much?
- Do you get your deposits back when you move out, and why or why not?
- What is the requirement for giving notice when you want to move (notice to vacate): Is it thirty days or sixty days?
- How many people can live in this apartment with you?

Shifting to the Business of Life

- What are the parking rules and regulations?
- Can you have pets (what kind and how many)?
- Are you required to obtain renter's insurance?
- What type of amenities or utilities are included in the rent such as use of laundry facilities, a pool, tennis courts, cost of water, trash, Internet/Wi-Fi, cable TV, etc.?
- Do you need separate keys or door codes to access any of the facilities?
- Is there a charge for lost keys? If so, how much?

Other Issues and Costs Related to Renting a House

- Find out who is responsible for maintaining the yard: Get it in writing on your rental agreement. Some landlords will hire a lawn service whose cost should be included in your rent. But, if you're doing the yard work, you will probably have to purchase tools such as a lawn mower and trimmer or edger. You can ask the landlord if he/she will reimburse you for the cost of the tools, unless you would prefer to own them.
- Are window coverings supplied, or will you have to purchase your own?
- Are there shower curtains, or will you have to purchase your own?
- Is there a washer and dryer in the house, or will you have to purchase your own?
- In case of an emergency, where are all the shut-off valves, connections or breakers for water, gas, and electricity? If something goes wrong with any of these you can call your landlord, or the utility company; but during evening or weekends hours, either or both might be hard to contact. So you should know this for your own safety.

- Is there a homeowner's association? If yes, find out the following things, and read more about these associations on Page 150. Are the association dues included in your rent or is that a separate charge?

  You should also get a copy of what is called the "CC & Rs" (Covenants, Conditions & Restrictions) which contains all the rules and restrictions for living in this neighborhood.

- Is there a community pool or other shared facilities such as tennis courts? If yes, do you need a key to access these things?

Purchasing a House

New vs. Used

Whether you buy a new house or an older house each has their pros and cons. Regardless of which way you go, I urge you to work with a real estate agent whom you know and trust.

While I have listed some things to watch for here, this is by no means a complete accounting of what can come up in a real estate transaction. You should also consider doing some research on the Internet (or talk with someone who is knowledgeable on the subject) to learn more about the whole process of buying a house or condominium. (Mobile homes are less complicated but have their own set of rules. In that case, be sure to work with an agent who specializes in mobile home sales.)

In either case, the amount of paperwork involved in a real estate transaction looks like it felled an entire forest, so again, work with someone (preferably an agent) you trust to guide you through the process.

New Houses/Condos

With a brand-new house, you get to pick out the lot on which it sits, the color of the carpet and a whole range of other things. But many things might not be included in the cost of the house:

- Window coverings
- Appliances such as refrigerator, microwave, washer and dryer
- A yard and/or a sprinkler system for that yard
- Trash cans (in some cities the trash company will supply these)
- Extra things you see in the model homes such as mirrors on closet doors, crown molding in the living room, built-in entertainment centers, fireplaces, granite countertops and glass-fronted cabinets in the kitchen.
- Warranties on the structure or the appliances (get the warranty information in writing along with who to call when you need to file a claim)

Be sure to ask about these things and if they are included, make sure that that is noted in one of the contracts or purchase agreements that your sign.

Also, be sure to read all the contracts and pieces of paper before you sign them.

The seller might want to rush you through the process by telling you that all these are "standard," documents, but most of us don't buy or sell a lot of houses, so there is no way for us to know exactly what is standard and what is not. Don't worry about looking stupid; this is how you protect yourself.

Bottom line, take your time and read everything regardless of how busy the seller is or how many other people are standing around waiting in the sales office.

Make notes and ask questions about anything you don't understand especially when it comes to dollar amounts. The only concession you might want to make is letting the salesperson know up front that you intend to read every document.

Home Loans

Unless you have a lot of cash in the bank, you will need to apply for a home loan. The length of the loan can vary from 15 to 30 years.

In order to increase your chances of getting approved for a loan, you will need to meet quite a few requirements specified by the lending bank. I've listed few things here that might be required, but you should check with your bank to learn its specific requirements.

- You must have held the same job for at least one year
- You need a good credit score (usually over 700)
- You will probably need cash to pay a percentage of the loan up front as a "down payment"

Fixed Rates vs. Variable Rates

This refers to the interest you will be charged. Interest is discussed in other sections of this handbook (Pages 91 and 102) so I won't redefine it here. However, I will explain how two other types of interest calculations work because they are the most common when it comes to home loans.

A "fixed" interest rate means that you will be charged the same percentage of interest throughout the entire loan.

For example, when you get a 30-year loan for 3 percent interest, you will always pay 3 percent interest on the balance owed on that loan, every month for 30 years. What the bank will do is set up the payments to be the same every month, but every month part of your payment goes toward the interest on the loan and part goes to the original loan (referred to as the "principle"), similar to a car loan (review the amortization chart on Page 157).

This is a very simplified explanation of how this works, so you should talk with your lender to learn more about the details. Bottom line, committing to (aka "locking in") a low interest rate for the entire length of the loan is the safest and best way to go financially speaking.

A "variable" interest rate means that the interest rate on your loan changes every few years. It might go up, it might go down. It's a gamble because it's based upon the general economy in your city, state or the whole country. Usually it's set up to have a lower rate for the first five years of the loan, such as 1.5 percent. This is fine if you plan on selling your home or property in that time frame.

Then, in the sixth year, the interest goes ("resets") to whatever your contract specifies: Read the fine print on this. It might be determined by the economy or it might be specified to go up to a rate of 3 percent for the next five years, and then 5 percent for the remainder of the loan.

But most "variable rate" loans are not that simple. Yes, in the first five years you'll get the 1.5 percent, but in the sixth year it might go to "1 percent over prime." "Prime" is the lowest interest rate charged to anyone with really good credit...that could be anywhere between 3 and 10 percent depending on the overall economy of the country. So now even if prime is only 4 percent, your interest rate will be one percent over prime, which is now 5 percent.

It doesn't sound too bad except when you realize that you were initially only paying 1.5 percent interest on that $150,000 loan. Now you have to pay 5 percent on whatever balance you still owe on that loan after five years. Do the math...your house payment could double.

> *__Note:__ Variable interest rates were really popular in the beginning of the 21st century. But millions of people lost their homes when those interest rates reset after five years: It caused their house payments to go up so high they could no longer afford them. No one could sell their houses fast enough so they just stopped making payments to the bank. As a result, the banks lost a lot of money in a very short amount of time. Therefore, they couldn't pay all their employees which started all the layoffs, thus the "economic crash" of 2008.*

Before you agree to and sign any loan document either do some math yourself or talk with someone who has done this before and who has your best interests at heart.

Property Taxes

In most states when you buy land, a house, or a condo, you are required to pay taxes on it every year. This makes me think of a sales tax that never ends. The county tax assessor will determine how much your property is worth (usually based upon what other property is selling for in the area, and the area's desirability), then do a calculation to come up with the amount you must pay every year.

If the value of your property goes down (maybe because the economy is bad), you can request a recalculation of the value and the taxes recalculated (aka, "reassessed"). On the other side of that coin, if the value goes up, then your taxes could be recalculated without your knowledge. You will receive the new bill in the mail.

Supplemental Property Taxes
When a builder of new homes first purchases the land on which he will eventually build homes, the amount of property tax is calculated on empty land. When a house is built on the land, it becomes more valuable, so the taxes go up. The difference between taxes paid on the empty lot, and the taxes paid on the lot with a house on it is called "supplemental property taxes." And you, the new homeowner, get to pay those taxes in the first tax year after you buy that house.

The first year in my first new house I got hit with a $2,800 supplemental tax bill – due upon receipt. Ask about this tax when you buy your new house.

When an existing house changes hands, the property value is also reassessed, therefore, this transaction might also prompt a supplemental tax bill. That should be a lower cost than the new home situation because the house was already there. However, when in doubt, ask!

Mello-Roos

When a new community is developed the city has to put in things such as new roads, streetlights, water lines and drainage, sewer systems and electrical lines that connect to the main "grid." Some cities in California have created Mello-Roo districts that issue bonds to pay for building this infrastructure. If you purchase a home in that community you get to pay for it in the form of taxes known as "Mello-Roos." (This tax, actually called the Community Facilities Act, was enacted in California in 1982 and is referred to as Mello-Roos because of its two co-authors Senator Harry J. Mello, and Assemblyman Mike Roos.)

Your Mello-Roo assessment will appear as a line item on your property tax bill every year for a limited number of years. Once all the new infrastructure is paid for, the tax is dropped from your bill.

If you are curious about how much these taxes are and where to find them on the bill, call the county tax assessor's office and ask.

Used Houses/Condos

In many cases a used home will already have a yard, carpets, window coverings and appliances. However, these things might not be the style, color or brands you prefer. In that case, be prepared to incur the extra cost of customizing all of them.

The other thing you need to consider is how old everything is and if there are any warranties. In many cases a seller might be required to pay for a one to ten year warranty to cover anything that breaks or fails within that time frame (this varies from state to state). Be sure to ask about it.

If there is no such requirement in your state, again, you must make a judgment call: How old is the plumbing or electrical wiring in the house? What about the appliances, such as the gas range and dishwasher? Do you have the extra money to pay for repairs or replacements?

Homeowner's Associations

Many communities have these clubs called "Homeowner's Associations," (HOA). If you purchase a home in a community with an HOA, you are required to join the organization and pay a monthly fee for maintenance and repairs of the common grounds within the community. Members of the HOA elect a governing board that decides what the rules and regulations are for living in this neighborhood, aka "community."

HOAs have a rule book, referred to as the "CC & Rs" which stands for "Community Covenants and Regulations."

Monthly dues can range from a low of $35 to $130, up to as much as $500 or even thousands of dollars a month, depending upon where you live and the amenities offered. The money is usually collected by (paid to) a management company on behalf of the association.

The HOA board generally consists of a president, a vice president, a secretary and a treasurer. These roles are held by volunteer (unpaid) homeowners who are voted in every year or two. Most associations will have monthly meetings to discuss or change the rules, consider any issues in the community, review applications received from someone wanting to change his or her landscaping, or to decide how money will be spent in the community. If you would like to add something to the agenda, you must check with the management company to find out how to go about doing so.

The purpose of the association is to make sure the neighborhood always looks nice and is a safe place in which to live. So there will be rules about maintaining your front yard (and sometimes backyards), the colors you can paint your home and overall repair of your house. The association will tow cars that sit in one place too long so the street in front of your house doesn't look like a used car lot.

The association dues might also pay for maintaining all the landscaping in shared areas of the neighborhood (such as parks or walkways and lighting); maintaining tennis courts, swimming pools (and pool furniture) or shared laundry facilities; any community clubhouses (along with its furniture); security guards and lifeguards.

When you decide to buy, or even rent, in a new area, be sure to ask if there is a homeowner's association, what the dues are, and how soon you can get a copy of the CC & Rs.

Homeowner's Insurance

When you apply for a home loan, the lender will require you purchase an insurance policy to cover any damage to the house for as long as you have the loan. This is another monthly cost that is added to your house payment. It is not optional.

Impound Accounts

If you have read all the related "Buying a House" sections up to this point, you now realize that there are a lot of monthly costs involved in buying a house: Homeowner's association dues, property taxes and homeowner's insurance. In some cases you can have your lender set up something called an "impound account."

This is basically a savings account for all these extra expenses that the bank will manage. It will calculate the monthly cost of your property taxes and homeowner's insurance, add it to your monthly house payment, and pay those two bills for you. This prevents you from having to worry about saving the money yourself throughout the year.

Also be aware that some lending banks require you do this.

Impound accounts usually don't include homeowner's association dues. Neither will they include supplemental property taxes (since those are just charged and paid within the first year in a new house).

If you would like to set up an impound account, or just learn more about it, talk with the lending bank when you apply for the loan.

Divorce

You file for divorce when you and your spouse decide that you can no longer live together peacefully. This is when you truly learn that a marriage is a financial arrangement.

Although I have been through three divorces of my own, I do not claim to be an expert on the topic. But I do know divorces can go one of two ways:

- **In a friendly divorce,** or one where there's really nothing (no real property, children or pets) to split between the two of you, you could just use a paralegal to assist with completing all the legal paperwork and filing it with the family courts.
- **In a nasty divorce** where there's a lot of fighting going on, I strongly suggest you consult a divorce lawyer in order to protect yourself and your finances.

In either situation, here are a few things to consider:

- **A friendly or "amicable" divorce (in California) will take a minimum of six months** from the minute you file the initial paperwork in family court. If it's an unfriendly or nasty divorce, it could take years. In either time frame a lot can happen.

- **In order to protect yourself financially, file for a legal separation immediately.** This will cut your responsibility for any debt your spouse incurs during the divorce proceedings.

  With a friendly divorce in which you are both talking to each other and working together to divide property, and are discussing money, alimony, child custody and child support, you probably don't need to do this. Only you can decide for sure.

- **Make copies of all bank account statements and credit card statements.** This will help both of you determine what debts (money owed) and assets (money and property owned) you share. When it comes to dividing it up, having these documents will make the discussion much easier, especially if one party empties the bank account without the other one's knowledge.

- **Close any joint credit cards as soon as possible.** This will protect both of you from one spouse running up more debt just to upset the other spouse. One of you can do this without the other's approval. You might want to be nice though, and let the other party know you are doing this to avoid him or her the embarrassment of using a closed credit card account in front of friends or coworkers.

- **Get copies of all retirement account statements.** Any funds added to these types of accounts during a marriage are considered community property.

- **Get copies of all pay stubs.** These are needed in cases where alimony and child support are determined.

- **If you own vehicles of any kind, a home, a business or any other property get it appraised.** Again, this aids in determining the value of community property and how it's to be divided between both parties.

This is by no means a complete list, just some suggestions to get you going in the right direction. You really should consult a divorce attorney to get all your questions answered.

Filing Income Taxes After a Divorce

You do have the option of filing taxes jointly for the last year in which you were still legally married. That said, it might not be the best choice for you financially or even emotionally. Talk to a tax professional to find out the best way to handle this.

Appendix A

Amortization Schedule

The following table is an example of how interest is charged on the car loan discussed on Page 103: The original principal is $21,300; the interest is 15 percent; the term is five years.

- The Interest column shows how much of the payment is interest.
- The Principal column shows how much of the payment is subtracted from the principal amount.

This chart shows that the interest is recalculated on the New Balance each month. Notice that each month, more of the payment is applied to the principal rather than the interest. After 60 months the principal is zero, therefore, the loan is paid off.

Payment #	Payment	Interest	Principal	New Balance
				$ 21,300.00
1	$506.73	$ 266.25	$240.48	$ 21,059.52
2	$506.73	$ 263.24	$ 243.48	$ 20,816.04
3	$506.73	$ 260.20	$ 246.52	$ 20,569.52
4	$506.73	$ 257.12	$ 249.61	$ 20,319.91
5	$506.73	$ 254.00	$ 252.73	$ 20,067.18
6	$506.73	$ 250.84	$ 255.89	$ 19,811.30
7	$506.73	$ 247.64	$ 259.08	$ 19,552.21
8	$506.73	$ 244.40	$ 262.32	$ 19,289.89
9	$506.73	$ 241.12	$ 265.60	$ 19,024.29
10	$506.73	$ 237.80	$ 268.92	$ 18,755.37
11	$506.73	$ 234.44	$ 272.28	$ 18,483.08
12	$506.73	$ 231.04	$ 275.69	$ 18,207.40
13	$506.73	$ 227.59	$ 279.13	$ 17,928.26
14	$506.73	$ 224.10	$ 282.62	$ 17,645.64
15	$506.73	$ 220.57	$ 286.15	$ 17,359.49
16	$506.73	$ 216.99	$ 289.73	$ 17,069.76
17	$506.73	$ 213.37	$ 293.35	$ 16,776.40
18	$506.73	$ 209.71	$ 297.02	$ 16,479.38

18	$506.73	$ 209.71	$ 297.02	$ 16,479.38
19	$506.73	$ 205.99	$ 300.73	$ 16,178.65
20	$506.73	$ 202.23	$ 304.49	$ 15,874.16
21	$506.73	$ 198.43	$ 308.30	$ 15,565.86
22	$506.73	$ 194.57	$ 312.15	$ 15,253.71
23	$506.73	$ 190.67	$ 316.05	$ 14,937.65
24	$506.73	$ 186.72	$ 320.00	$ 14,617.65
25	$506.73	$ 182.72	$ 324.00	$ 14,293.64
26	$506.73	$ 178.67	$ 328.05	$ 13,965.59
27	$506.73	$ 174.57	$ 332.16	$ 13,633.43
28	$506.73	$ 170.42	$ 336.31	$ 13,297.12
29	$506.73	$ 166.21	$ 340.51	$ 12,956.61
30	$506.73	$ 161.96	$ 344.77	$ 12,611.84
31	$506.73	$ 157.65	$ 349.08	$ 12,262.77
32	$506.73	$ 153.28	$ 353.44	$ 11,909.33
33	$506.73	$ 148.87	$ 357.86	$ 11,551.47
34	$506.73	$ 144.39	$ 362.33	$ 11,189.13
35	$506.73	$ 139.86	$ 366.86	$ 10,822.27
36	$506.73	$ 135.28	$ 371.45	$ 10,450.83
37	$506.73	$ 130.64	$ 376.09	$ 10,074.74
38	$506.73	$ 125.93	$ 380.79	$ 9,693.94
39	$506.73	$ 121.17	$ 385.55	$ 9,308.39
40	$506.73	$ 116.35	$ 390.37	$ 8,918.02
41	$506.73	$ 111.48	$ 395.25	$ 8,522.77
42	$506.73	$ 106.53	$ 400.19	$ 8,122.58
43	$506.73	$ 101.53	$ 405.19	$ 7,717.39
44	$506.73	$ 96.47	$ 410.26	$ 7,307.13
45	$506.73	$ 91.34	$ 415.39	$ 6,891.74
46	$506.73	$ 86.15	$ 420.58	$ 6,471.16
47	$506.73	$ 80.89	$ 425.84	$ 6,045.33
48	$506.73	$ 75.57	$ 431.16	$ 5,614.17
49	$506.73	$ 70.18	$ 436.55	$ 5,177.62
50	$506.73	$ 64.72	$ 442.01	$ 4,735.62
51	$506.73	$ 59.20	$ 447.53	$ 4,288.09
52	$506.73	$ 53.60	$ 453.12	$ 3,834.96
53	$506.73	$ 47.94	$ 458.79	$ 3,376.17
54	$506.73	$ 42.20	$ 464.52	$ 2,911.65
55	$506.73	$ 36.40	$ 470.33	$ 2,441.32
56	$506.73	$ 30.52	$ 476.21	$ 1,965.11
57	$506.73	$ 24.56	$ 482.16	$ 1,482.95
58	$506.73	$ 18.54	$ 488.19	$ 994.76
59	$506.73	$ 12.43	$ 494.29	$ 500.47
60	$506.73	$ 6.26	$ 500.47	$ (0.00)
	$ 30,403.53	$ 9,103.53	$ 21,300.00	

Shifting to the Business of Life

- The second column shows the total of payments made: $30,403.53. That is the total cost of the loan.
- The third column shows the amount of interest paid on the loan: $9,103.53

Again, these numbers can help you to understand the benefit of having a lower interest rate.

Appendix B

Balancing a Checkbook

How Often

This is something you should do every month if you have a checkbook and you pay for things with a combination of online payments, paper checks, and a debit card. Although you keep track of all your transactions in a checkbook register (yes, you should do this unless you are a mathematical genius and can keep track of everything in your head), you never know when any of these transactions will be deducted from your checking account. So balancing your account once a month reassures you that the balance you see in your register matches up with what the bank says you have.

It is very easy to make a mathematical error that overdraws your account and not even notice it until after you rack up $300 in overdraft fees. Balancing your checkbook will help you to catch those errors sooner rather than later.

When

Generally you should balance your checkbook within a day or two of receiving a statement in the mail (or online).

Preparation

Before you begin, set aside at least one hour of quiet time. Get a cup of coffee, tea or ice water and some sort of calculator. (I do my calculations in an Excel spreadsheet.) Now open the statement and read the instructions on the back.

I've described generally how it's done here, but if you have any difficulty with this process you can always go to the bank and ask for assistance. Do this when you get the first statement for your new account. Do not walk into the bank with six months worth of statements and ask for help: They will laugh out loud and send you on your merry way.

Steps

This is basically what it says:

1. Compare the list of transactions on the statement to the transactions you wrote in your checkbook register.

2. If the item on the statement is in your checkbook, then put a check mark next to it in both places: On the statement so you know it's in your checkbook, and in the checkbook so you remember that it's on the statement. That means that the bank already deducted it from your account (checks, online payments, ATM withdrawals or debit card transactions) or added it in (deposits such as payroll checks or other checks).

3. Look back through the register and find all the deposits that did not show up on the statement. There is a place on the back of the statement where you can write these in.

4. Add them up and write in the total where it tells you to. This is referred to as your "outstanding deposits/credits."

5. Look back through the register again and find all the checks, online payments, ATM withdrawals or debit card transactions that did not show up on the statement. There is another place on the back of the statement where you can write these in too.

6. Add them up at the bottom and write in the total where it tells you to. These are referred to as "outstanding checks/debits."

7. Now read the instructions and find the place where it tells you to "enter the statement ending balance here" and write it there (that number is usually located on the front of the first page of the statement).

This is the math

8. Add the "ending balance" to the "outstanding deposits." Now you have a subtotal.

9. Next, take the "subtotal " and subtract the "outstanding checks." This number is the "bank balance."

10. Compare the "bank balance" to the balance in your checkbook: They should be exactly the same. That means that your checkbook balanced. Yay!

If the bank balance and your checkbook balance do not match, there are quite a few reasons this can happen:

- Redo steps two, three and five (listed on the previous page) which is rechecking to make sure you noted all credits and debits that did or did not appear on the statement. (This is usually where I find that I forgot to list a check as outstanding.)

- Double-check the math you did when adding up all the outstanding debits (checks, debit cards, online payments and ATM withdrawals) and credits (deposits).
- Check the math on each transaction in your checkbook to see if there is a mathematical error somewhere.

In most cases you will find the error after completing either one or more of the steps above.

If you don't, I suggest you sleep on it and come back to it in the morning with a fresh set of eyes.

If you still cannot find the error, you can ask a friend or relative for help, or you can ask your bank. Some banks offer this assistance for free; some will charge a fee.

Appendix C

Supplies for Your First Apartment

This is a quick list of the basics you might not want to be without in your first new apartment. To personalize this list and make it more complete, walk around your current home with a printed copy of it and add to it as you spot things that would be "nice to have."

Kitchen

- Kitchen table & chairs
- Dishwashing sponge/cloths
- Dishwashing liquid soap
- If you have a dishwasher you also need detergent for that
- Hand soap for washing hands
- Hand towels
- Dish drying towels
- Pot holders
- A set of dishes: Dinner plates/bowls/small plates/coffee cups
- A set of glasses
- A set of silverware

Food Prep Tools:

- Frying pan with lid
- 3-4 pots in small to large sizes with lids
- 3-4 mixing bowls
- Glass baking dishes
- Wooden mixing spoons
- Serving spoons/forks
- Containers for leftovers
- Small appliances
- Toaster or toaster oven
- Coffeemaker
- Microwave (if none installed)
- Crock pot (not required, just nice to have)

First Aid Kit

The kitchen is usually where you get most cuts, burns and bruises. Look on the Internet for a list of things you should keep in your first-aid kit and keep it in your kitchen.

Food

Make a "menu" of what you will have for three meals a day (seven days a week), plus snacks and drinks. (Everyone snacks, so don't skip this.)

As you make that menu, think of any storage containers you might need for bulk items such as flour, pasta, sugar, salt, pepper or other spices.

Bathroom

- Plumber's Helper (toilet plunger)
- For one person get two each of the following, for two people, get four each of the following. That way you have a clean towel when the dirty one is in the laundry basket.
- 2 Hand/face towels
- 2 Bath towels
- 2 Wash cloths- optional use in the shower
- Personal preference; You might use a loofa instead.

Personal use items

- Toilet paper
- Toothpaste
- Floss
- A drinking cup
- Shampoo/conditioner
- Shower soap or gel
- Hand soap or gel for the sink
- Comb
- Brush

Optional Items
- Hair dryer
- Curling Iron
- Hair styling products
- Scale (to watch yourself lose weight, as you might not have a huge food budget when you first move out)
- A rug to put next to the bathtub or shower (prevents slipping on wet tile when stepping out of the shower)

Living room
- Sofa and/or chairs for you and guests
- TV/ DVD Player
- TV stand (or mounting brackets for wall-mounted TV)
- Lamp (s)
- End table for the lamps (bedroom/living room)

Bedroom
- Bed
- Dresser
- Nightstand
- Alarm clock
- Lamp
- 2 Sets of sheets (1 to use, 1 to wash)
- Blankets and/or comforter
- 1 or 2 Pillows
- Clothes hangars

General
- Light bulbs for all rooms (kitchen, bath, living room)
- Laundry basket
- Supply of quarters for the pay-as-you-go washing machines
- Decorative pillows & blankets for those nights when you fall asleep watching TV
- Any family photos or other decorative items (doilies) to put on the wall, counter, kitchen table or end tables
- Trash cans

Shifting to the Business of Life

Cleaning Supplies

- Vacuum cleaner
- Broom & dust pan
- scrubbing sponges
- "Soft Scrub" for cleaning porcelain surfaces
- Toilet bowl brush
- Window/mirror cleaner
- Dust rags – old T-shirts work fine
- Furniture polish for dusting
- Floor cleaner
- Mop & bucket- optional but nice to have

Tools

In the case of small repairs around the house, ask your landlord for assistance: This is his or her job. That said, if you have the landlord's written permission to hang pictures and TVs on the wall and would like to do it yourself, you might consider purchasing the following tools:

- Flat head and Phillips screwdrivers
- Hammer
- Electric drill (you'd be surprised how handy this is)
- Picture hangers
- Box of small nails, large nails, and screws in various sizes
- A level (to make sure the pictures are hung straight)
- Channel lock pliers (ask at any hardware store)

Tip: *If you are not a "handy, fix-it" kind of person, you might want to find a handy man (or ask your landlord) to deal with the kind of repairs that require some of the tools listed above.*

Appendix D

Supplies for Your First House

When you buy or rent a house, you will need all the same items listed in the previous Appendix C, "Supplies for Your First Apartment." So print out that list and then take a look at the items below.

Houses don't always include things like window coverings and they usually come with a yard so you might also need a few other things:

- Window Coverings (curtains or blinds)
- Appliances such as refrigerator, microwave, washer and dryer

Yard Tools
- Lawn mower
- Weed-whacker/edger
- Tools for removing weeds: Gloves, small shovel

Final Thoughts

Everything you do has a price to pay: Good or bad, right or wrong.

All your decisions and actions will have an effect on you, and possibly the ones you love along with anyone else in your world. So be sure to think everything through before you act. And always have a "Plan B" just in case your original plan doesn't work out.

Sincerely,
Janet M. Nast

Made in the USA
Charleston, SC
23 March 2015